GRAIN in BRICS
Emerging Technologies in Emerging Economies

Dr. Syed Afzal Murtaza Rizvi

Dr. Halima Sadia Rizvi

Khanna Book Publishing Co. (P) Ltd.

Delhi

ISBN: 978-93-80016-12-2

First Impression, 2010

Published by:
Khanna Book Publishing Co. (P) Ltd.
1694-95, Nai Sarak, Delhi-110006 (India)
Phone: 011-23283211, 23256658
Fax: 011-23256658
E-mail: contact@khannaedu.com
Website: www.khannaedu.com

Cover Design & Layout by
Limited Colors

Printed in India by
S.K. Printer (Delhi)

GRAIN in BRICS Emerging Technologies in Emerging Economies

PREFACE

The power of ideas in transforming human civilizations is unquestionable. Ideas when transformed into inventions and then to innovations have produced leaps and bound revolutionary results, be they the discovery of fire, the invention of the wheel or the knowledge of money. What rules the world is the wealth, strength and the power of the ideas. Many such ideas which have been responsible for drastically bringing about change into the economic world of some countries such as the BRICS (Emerging Economies: **B**razil, **R**ussia, **I**ndia, **C**hina and **S**outh Africa) and transform them from developing to future super economic powers have been the emerging technologies of GRAIN (Emerging Technologies: **G**enetic Engineering, **R**obotics, **A**rtificial Intelligence, **I**nformation Technology, **N**ano Technology).

Credit rating agencies predict and foresee the future of these BRICS economies very bright and may even surpass the so called developed nations. These economies have not only the ideas and inventions in the use of GRAIN but they also have to their advantage a prominent natural resource in the form of human capital. These economies have been effectively utilizing this important resource which at times was considered as a major hurdle in their growth process. An all responsible element for slowing down their growth rates have shown to the world that it is ideas and thereby development of technologies which can transform demographic doom to demographic boom.

There is a dire need to critically examine and evaluate this co-relation, develop analysis and suggest measures all the more in the present day global slow down context.

While developed industrial countries such as the US and UK have become vulnerable to global slowdown, the extent of shock resistance /

absorption witnessed and the bearing capacity of these emerging economies is enormous. Reasons being the firm groundings in attaining growth rates which are associated with real sector such as agriculture-for India and Brazil, and manufacturing for China, than artificially created or simulated hyped values of real estates or exchange rates which have transformed into bubbles through sub-prime transactions.

The book is an Ernest attempt in examining the role of emerging technologies which have been instrumental in bringing about transformational changes to these economies. For example, Brazil has effectively used genetically modified corn which is the basic ingredient for ethanol production. Similarly India and China have successfully transformed their human resource into knowledge based, skillful, literate and trained computer/information technology professionals whose contribution both in terms of foreign exchange earnings and employment generations have been enormous. Russia is a leading inventor, producer and exporter of robotic technology. Nanotechnology is also finding its place by enormous extent in these economies. It is this combination which reveals how and why these emerging economies are going to be important superpowers in the process of decision making and affecting the lives of 40% of the world's population.

This book intends to provide an essential tool to a wide range of professionals not only in the field of economic analysis and policy makers besides general audience and students of Economics and Management Studies. It is equally an important ready reference and analytical material to professionals such as Genetic Engineers, Robotics Engineers, Computer and Information Technologists and Nano Technologists.

For the sake of clarity of understanding and purpose the study is broadly classified into six sections.

The introduction provides motivation for the main models presented in the book. It is devoted exclusively to give the audience a subtle feel of the various aspects of emerging economies and the concepts, terminology and fundamental characteristics of different emerging technologies are also discussed.

The book is spread over Seven chapters, Chapter one is for Introduction and the Chapter VII is for Conclusion. The Five Chapters from II to VI deals each country, exclusively, viz., The Chapter II is devoted for Brazil, Chapter III is for Russia, Chapter IV is for India, Chapter V is for China, and Chapter VI is for South Africa.. The Final Chapter VII is the conclusion.

The Chapter II devotes to the first of the BRICS i.e., the Emerging Economy of Brazil. The study sets out with discussing the Geography; History, Geo-political advantages, the Economic structure, the major competitive advantages in production process as well as the role of FDI in Brazil are cited in detail.

The role of emerging technologies in various sectors of Brazil is examined in detail in the second part of the section.

Chapter III deals the Emerging Economy of Russia. This chapter gives a detailed account of Russian history and the break down of the erstwhile USSR. Along with the politics and government structure, an analysis of the economy includes the state of the environment as well as the health of its people. The change of Russia from a closed economy into a more mixed one through the process of privatization is also traced. Russia is also the only country among the BRICS that is not a part of the World Trade Organization. The section presents the reasons of the opposition and the position of the country. The second part of the Russian section traces the development of the emerging technologies in the nation. As mentioned earlier, Russia has made massive development in robotics and information technology.

The Chapter IV of the study deals with India. After a brief recount of the Indian history, the section deals with the main resource of India- its population. A large part of this population depends on agriculture, though all other sectors are growing fast as well. Here the role played by financial institution and Foreign Direct Investment is analyzed. In India the emerging technologies are making fast progress. Genetically modified crops are already been planted and studied in various parts of the country; India is already known for its information technology services across the world. In the fields of nanotechnology and robotics- development is taking place in leaps and bounds.

The Chapter V covers the emerging economy of China. China has also moved from a communist regime to a more open economy. After tracing the history of the country, the study emphasis the population control programme Although the programme has resulted in an aging population in China, the government has already taken steps to ensure that the problem is dealt with soon. The sectoral study examines the agricultural, industrial and Foreign Investment as well. China is making tremendous strides in the technological field. The emerging technologies section examines how all the GRAIN technologies have been encouraged by the government resulting in a well developed base for an economic superpower.

Chapter VI examines the rise of the Republic of South Africa into an Emerging Economy. With its history of racial discrimination, the country has witnessed a tremendous rise into the world economy within a short span of time. The country has huge potential in terms of natural resources and human capital. South Africa has been an addition to the emerging economies but has proved that it has all the makings of an economic superpower. The section examines closely the various sectors of the economy – agriculture, industry, the financial institutions and the foreign direct investments. As the country was a late entrant into the world economy, the technologies have yet to play an important role in the economy. However, some steps have been taken such as genetic crops, information technologies etc. The potential for future impact on the economy is untapped and waited to be realized.

Each of the sections on the emerging economies cross checks the major economies strengths and linkages of the economy with the technologies.

Chapter VII provides comprehensive conclusive framework for these economies. A general conclusion for all emerging economies and emerging technologies reveal that these economies are here to stay and control major economic and socio-political powers.

The Appendix notes various important statistical tables and detailed bibliography and the selected list of references.

This creative work has been an important task in itself. Its one of the culminations of a great ides, a constant persistent effort, a regular search for details, numerous discussions, various suggestions and ultimately a substantial sweat of sincere, hard and devoted effort by two pure souls, ourselves, assisted by a sincere and charming research scholar, Ms Sahana Andrew. Motivated by two ideal souls, Ms Neda Fatima, our daughter, and Mr Bilal, our son, for whom we are epitomes of perfections. We hope we have lived up to their expectations.

Dr Syed Afzal Murtaza Rizvi
Dr Halima Sadia Rizvi

CONTENTS

INTRODUCTION

The term emerging economies was first used by Antoine W van Agtmael in 1981 to describe the fast growing economies with low to middle per capita income. Such countries constitute about 80% of the global population, representing 20% of the world's economies. Although a loose definition, countries in this category vary from very small to big economies, are considered emerging due to their development and reforms. Thus China, considered a powerhouse is clubbed together with Tunisia, a country with very little resources. Both the countries are called emerging economies as they have embarked on economic development and reforms and have begun to open their markets to 'emerge' into the global scene.

In the 1960's and 1970's, development economists often compared the future development possibilities for India and China- the world's most populous countries and Brazil, Latin America's largest economy. Under the Communists regime, China had invested heavily in the health and education of its people and forcibly limited population growth. Following the Soviet model, China and India had based their economic development on heavy industralisation protected from international competition by high tariff walls. Brazil followed a similar strategy of import substitution industralisation.

By the end of the Cold War or even before, the countries initiated the economic and political reforms to allow their countries to enter the world economy. In order to compete, the countries have simultaneously stressed education, foreign investment, domestic consumption and domestic entrepreneurship.

In 2003, Jim O'Neil of Goldman Sachs investigated the economic growth of four countries- Brazil, Russia, India and China and came up with the acronym BRIC. It was shown in the study that these countries would exceed the GDP (PPP) of the current developed countries within the next 40 years. According to the study, India has the potential to grow the fastest among the BRICs mainly because the decline in working age population will happen later for India and Brazil than for Russia and China.

Although the BRIC economies are not yet the most important and largest economies in the world, they already play an important role in many economic spheres such as demanding changes in the subsidy policies of the developing countries and signing treaty among themselves. It is no longer possible to ignore these countries in world decisions. Hence it becomes imperative to study these countries in their historical background to understand their present and future aspects of growth and development.

The report published by Goldman Sachs, titled 'Dreaming with BRICs-The Path to 2050' predicted that over the next few decades the growth generated by the developing countries especially the BRIC countries (Brazil, Russia, India and China) could become a much larger force than it is now. The main conclusions are in five areas:

(a) **Economic size** in less than 40 years the BRIC economies together could be larger than G 6 (US, UK, Japan, France, Italy, Germany) in US dollar terms. By 2025 they could account for over half the size of G 6. Currently they are worth less than 15%. In US dollar terms China could overtake Germany in next four years, Japan by 2015 and the US by 2039.

(b) **Economic growth:** Of the BRIC economies, India has the potential for the fastest growth in the next 30 to 50 years.

(c) **Incomes and demographics:** China's per capita income could be similar to where the developed countries are now.

Demographic trends also affect the way the world changes. The effects however vary greatly. The decline in working age population is generally projected to take place later than in developed countries but will be steeper in Russia and China than in India and Brazil.

(d) **Global demand patterns** as early as 9, the annual increase in US dollars spending from the BRIC could be greater than that from G and four times higher by 2050.

(e) **Currency movement:** BRICs real exchange rate could appreciate up to 300% over the next 50 years (an average of 2.5 % per year)

The potential for such growth rate comes from two sources: First, developing countries have less capital per worker than the developed countries. Returns on capital are higher because it tends to have a bigger impact in the early stages of development than later on and a given investment rate results in higher growth in capital stock. A single road does more to open up an area than an extra road within an existing dense network. Secondly when developing countries invest, they move from nowhere to the state of the art equipment, whereas the developed economies get productivity gains more slowly.

A set of core factors can set the stage for growth such as:

(a) **Macro stability:** an unstable macro environment can hamper growth by distorting prices and incentive. Inflation hinders growth by discouraging savings and investment. A key focus therefore is price stability achieved through deficit reduction, tighter monetary policy and exchange rate realignment

(b) **Institutions:** more efficient institutions allow an economy to produce same output with fewer inputs. Institutions in this board sense include legal systems, functioning market health and education system financial institutions and government bureaucracy. Each of the BRIC is likely to face challenges in the political development in the next few decades.

(c) **Openness:** openness to trade and FDI can provide access to imported inputs new technology and larger markets

(d) **Education:** As the economies grow rapidly, they may face shortages of skilled workers. This means that more years of schooling is a prerequisite for the next stage of development. The long run estimates of the report are based on a strong connection between secondary education and growth potential. Of the BRICs India has the most work to do in expanding education.

The investment theory of decoupling suggests that the economic performance of the emerging economies of Brazil, Russia, India and China and of Asia in general, is now largely disconnected from that of the developing world. Statistically, China now accounts for a substantial portion of total world economic growth and most of that growth results from increased demand for Goods and Services within China itself. Trade among Asian economies is increasing more rapidly than trade between these economies and the rest of the world. As a result the setbacks to growth expected in America and perhaps Europe will have little impact on emerging economies markets.

The growth of BRIC countries is a result of the changes that occurred there. The western countries did not create the momentum for growth in these countries, nor can they stop their gradual transition into the developed world. Countries are masters of their own destiny because they are masters of their own economic, political and social institutions. Reducing global poverty is not about fairer distribution of finite resources. It is about every country's ability to make the effective use of its principal resource-its human talent.

According to the BRIC thesis, China and India will become world's dominant suppliers of manufactured goods and services respectively while Brazil and Russia will become suppliers of raw materials. These countries are not a political alliance like EU, or any formal trading association-but they have the potential to form a powerful economic block.

Among the four economies of BRIC- China and India seem to have the competitive edge. These two countries are competing with the world for 'intellectual capital'- investing in technology and education as well as using their expatriate citizens to generate business in the home country. Russia and Brazil on the other hand have not invested in the same way. Russia's natural resources are increasingly concentrated in state hands, which put off foreign investors. Brazil is slow to make changes that would positively affect the economic outlook across a broad range of sectors. Both countries have poor infrastructure systems. According to a study conducted by BT, India is perceived as the most comfortable to do business among the BRIC economies, China is rated next while Russia is considered the least comfortable.

Economist have also included another country to these four emerging economies- South Africa, thereby BRICS becomes the new acronym for these emerging economies. The economies of BRICS are worth approximately $3.186trillion (2002) in GDP and account for about 9% of world's GDP. While these figures may not be large, they account for a large share of the world's population and land area approximately 29.7% of the total land area (3,973 sq. km) and approximately 43.3% of the world's population (2.7 billion people). Moreover these five countries have something else in common- they are endowed with natural resources. In recent times the BRICS have been taking advantage of their abundant resources and achieving steady economic growth. However the countries are at different stages of their growth process. In the following section we look at each of these five countries to study the factors underlying its economic growth.

EMERGING TECHNOLOGIES

In an ever-changing world, technologies are been invented all over the world at tremendous speed. In 2002, Douglas Mulhall wrote about how five technologies are going to transform the world. He called it 'Our Molecular Future'. Genetic technology, Robotics, Artificial Intelligence and Nanotechnology (GRAIN) are here to stay. The scope of each of these technologies is wide and the development occurring in it is huge. Some parts of these technologies are still debated and mired in controversies. Therefore it is not possible to have a complete account of them here. However an attempt is made to briefly introduce and explain the significance of these emerging technologies to each of the emerging economies.

Genetic technology

Considered as one the most important discoveries of the 20th century is the discovery by James Watson and Francis Crick- the structure of the DNA molecule, which is the basis of heredity. While Darwin showed how evolution was a slow natural process, Watson and Crick showed how the process can be made to move much faster in the direction we want it to move. Genetic engineering refers to the whole range of technologies that depend on the direct manipulation of DNA. The technology provides us with the potential to improve health, create a safe and secure food supply and attain a sustainable environment. The application of the technology in the fields of biomedicine, agriculture, food production and processing has evoked strong public response.

Genes are made from a chemical called DNA-deoxyribonucleic acid. These are in turn made up of four bases- A, T, C, and G- that is repeated billions of times. The particular pattern of the bases is very important as it underlines all life's diversity. It was then discovered that parts of genes could be extracted from DNA, then copied or cloned. Transferring single genes between different plants and animals by turning the gene "switches" up or down or removing the gene and placing it in a different position in the same organism- all refer to gene. Plants, animals or microbes that have a new gene inserted into them are called Genetically Modified Organisms (GMO) or transgenic.

In order to address the important issue of world hunger and food security the Food and Agricultural Organization at the 2002 World Summit had formally endorsed Biotechnology as a way to eradicate hunger and malnutrition. GM foods have spread world wide ever since. According to a study by CI-ROAF the global area under GM crops increased from 1.7 million hectares in 1996 to 81.0 million hectares in 2004. About 80% of the crops are planted in two countries- United States and Argentina. Together with Canada and Brazil- they account for 91% of GM crops acreage. The remaining GM acreage is accounted for by two countries- China with 3.7 million hectares of GM cotton and Paraguay with 1.2 million hectares of GM crops. These six countries therefore account for almost all GM production in the world. According to ISAAA, the area under biotech crops is growing at a rate of 12%. The number of countries planting biotech crops has increased to 23-including 12 developing countries. In order of hectare- USA, Argentina, Brazil, Canada, India, China, Paraguay, South Africa, Uruguay, Philippines and so on. Of these, the first eight countries grew more than 1 million hectares each. The accumulated hectarage from 1996 to 2007 exceeded 2/3rd of a billion i.e. 169 million hectares a 67 fold increase between the years. Another milestone achieved in 2007 was that the number of small and resource-poor farmers benefiting from biotech crops in developing countries exceeded 10 million. Of the global total of 12 million beneficiary farmers, over 90% or 11 million were small and resource-poor farmers from developing countries—7.1 million in China (Bt cotton), 3.8 million in India (Bt cotton) and the rest 100,000 in Philippines (biotech maize), South Africa (biotech cotton, maize, soybean) and other eight developing countries.

Most of the GM technology is owned by a single company Monsato. In 2001, the products of Monsato account for 91% of their total area sown.

Robotics is the science of robots, their design, manufacture and applications. Although the capabilities of robots greatly differ, they all share the features of a mechanical movable structure under some form of control. The IFR statistical department in its World Robotic survey, 2007 has stated that in 2007 there were 951000 robotic worldwide of which 50% is in Asia, one-third in Europe, 16% in North America, Australasian and Africa each share 1% of the total. Although the automotive and electronic industries reduced their investment in robotics by 17% and 34% respectively, all other industrial sectors increased their robotic investment by 25%. In Asia robotic sales fell by 19% in 2006. However in China, India, Malaysia and Taiwan, the sector was performing well. China is now the third largest Asian market grew by 29% since 2006. In India robotic sales have doubled. In the last decade, the performance of the robots has increased tremendously, while at the same time the prices have decreased. A robot sold in 2002 would have cost less than a fifth of what a robot with the same performance would have cost in 1990. In the last few years the price decrease has started to level off. Profitability studies have shown that it is not unusual for robots to have pay back period as short as one to two years. According to Jan Karlsson, "The falling or stable robot prices, the increasing labour cost and continuously improving technology are the major driving forces which speak for continued massive robotic investment in the industry." Robots are now used in all fields-be it medical robots, underwater robots, surveillance robots, demolition robots or any of the numerous applications of the technology. In the long run, these service robots will not only mow our lawns and clean our floors but will carry out surgery, inspect pipes and handle hazardous materials for us, fight fires, detect bombs and also assist old and handicapped people with sophisticated interactive equipment. Robots have been widely used in surgery. One of the robots is called the Da Vinci Surgical System developed by Intuitive Surgical. The robot enables the surgeon to see the surgical site in clearer detail than the human eye. The system uses three stainless steel rods held in place by robotic arms. Using joystick like movements the surgeon can remotely operate on the patient.

Artificial Intelligence is defined as the study and design of intelligent agents. The intelligent agent is a system that perceives its environment and takes actions which maximizes its chances of success. According to John Mc Carthy, who coined the term in 1956, AI is the science and engineering of making intelligent machines especially intelligent computer programmes. It is similar to using computers to understand human intelligence. Computer programmes have the speed and ability but their ability corresponds to the intellectual mechanisms that programme designers have understood well enough to put it in the programme. Some abilities that children do not develop until they reach their teen years may be in the programmes while some abilities possessed by two-year old, may not be in them. The problem becomes more complicated by the fact that cognitive sciences have not been able to determine exactly what the human abilities are. After World War II many researchers started to work on intelligent machines. Considered as one of the forerunners Alan Turing said that AI was best researched by programming the computer rather than on building machines. He said that if a machine could act as intelligently as a human being then it is as intelligent as a human being. Samuel Butler raised the possibility of a "Mechanical Consciousness" that emerges as Darwinian evolution. According to McCorduck, AI in one form or another is an idea that has pervaded intellectual history, a dream in urgent need to be realized.

Nanotechnology is defined as the engineering of functional systems at the molecular scale. A nanometer is one-billionth or 10^{-9} of a meter. There are two main approaches to nanotechnology. One is the 'bottom-up' approach where materials and devices are built from molecular components which assemble themselves chemically by principles of molecular recognition. In the 'top-down' approach nano-objects are constructed from larger entities without atomic-level control.

When K. Eric Drexler popularized the word 'nanotechnology' in the 1980's, he was talking about building machines on the scale of molecules. Nanotechnology is sometimes referred to as a 'general- purpose technology'. In its advanced form, it will have significant impact on almost all industries and all areas of society. The technology will offer better built, longer lasting, cleaner, safer and smater products for homes, communications, medicine, agriculture and for industry in general.

The GRAIN technologies thus have a tremendous impact on the future of the world. The BRICS are at the brink of becoming superpowers—all of them already making their presence felt in different ways and the one that succeeds would be the one that is able to make full use of these technologies. Goldman Sach's prediction will need to account for the strengths and weakness of the emerging economies on the basis of these emerging technologies.

1 BRAZIL

Capital	—	Brasilia
Area	—	8,511,965 sq. km
Population	—	196,342,592 (July 2008 estimate)
Average rate of growth of	—	1.228% population

Currency	—	real (BRL)
GDP(PPP)	—	$ 1.849 trillion(2007)
GDP (per capita PPP)	—	$ 9,500 (2007)
GDP real growth rate	—	5.4% (2007)
Agriculture as a share of GDP	—	5.5% (2007)
Exports	—	$160.6 billion (2007)
Life Expectancy at birth	—	71.71 years (2008)
Infant mortality rate	—	23.33 deaths/1000 live birth (2008 est.)
Literacy	—	88.6% (2004)
Human Development Index	—	0.800 ranked 70th

In the past few decades, Brazil has experienced periods of high economic growth rates, and at the same time, problems of poverty, unemployment and extreme income inequality have emerged to be serious problems. Brazil is the fifth largest nation in terms of the geographical area and also the fifth most populous country as well. It occupies nearly half the total area of South America. To the north, west and south the country borders almost every South American country except Ecuador and Chile. To the east it is bound by the Atlantic Ocean with a coastline of more than 13, 490 kms. Although the country is the fifth most populous nation, the majority of its people live in the urban area and the coastlines. As we move to the interior of the country the population less dense. The average density of population is 22 per sq. km.

Due to the increased urbanization, the country is facing the problem associated with it -the growth of slums. The falevas of Rio de Janeiro and other such slums lack the basic facilities of clean water, electricity and sewage system. These settlements account for more than 60% of the urban population. The problem of inequality is another persistent problem in Brazil. The Gini coefficient, that measures the level of inequality in the countries of the world shows that Brazil has one of the highest levels of inequality in the world. Inequality increased from 0.57 in 1981 to 0.63 in 1989. Currently it is estimated to be 0.56 in 2004. The richest 10% of the population receive about 48% of the national income while the poorest 20% receive only 2.5% As in the case of other developing countries, the cities of Brazil are unable to create enough jobs for the large population. Consequently unemployment is high and people resort to activities like street vending, drug peddling, etc. Incomes are much lower in this informal sector and many people struggle to obtain enough to survive.

The country is rich in flora and fauna as both the Equator and the Tropic of Capricorn pass through its lands. Forests that include the largest rain forest in the world cover about one half of Brazil. Brazil's terrains include the dense forests, semiarid scrubland, hills and mountains, plains and a large coastal strip. Unfortunately, most of its soil has little agricultural value-only 6.93% of its land is arable.[1]

Brazil is unique in the Americas because, after its independence from Portugal, it did not fragment into separate countries as did the British and Spanish possessions in the region; rather it retained its identity through the intervening centuries and a variety of forms of government. Due to this hegemony, the Portuguese language is universal except among the Brazilian native Indians, especially in the remote Amazon basin.

1.1 BRIEF HISTORY

When the Portuguese arrived in Brazil in 1500, the natives were mainly semi nomadic living along the banks of the major rivers and the coasts of the country. In the beginning the Portuguese did not have much interest in the country due to their profitable trade with Indochina. Later, after 1530, they began to take efforts to have more effective control over their colony. Several settlements began to be established such as the capital Salvador. The Portuguese adopted an economy based on the production of agricultural goods that was exported to Europe. Sugar was the most important colonial product until the early 18th century. During the 18th century, gold and diamond deposits were found in the state of Minas Gerais.

1 World fact Book –Brazil

The mines helped to finance the Portuguese Royal Court Debts. The locals were however heavily burdened with taxes leading to popular movements supporting independence from the taxes of the colonial government. The movements such as the Tiradentes in 1789 and others were suppressed by the regime.

Although other imperialist countries, particularly the Dutch and French powers threatened the colony, the Portuguese administration kept the territorial, political and linguistic integrity. Portugal had even send bullion to Brazil, a spectacular reversal of colonial trend, in order to protect the nation from other foreign attacks.

In 1808, the Portuguese established themselves in the city of Rio de Janeiro, which became the seat of the entire government of Portugal until 1821. After Joao VI returned to Portugal in 1821, his heir apparent, Pedro became the regent of the Kingdom of Brazil. Brazil achieved her independence from Portugal after a series of political incidences and disputes. On December 1, 1822, Dom Pedro was crowned the first Emperor of Brazil. Pedro government was however considered to be politically and administratively inefficient. Political pressures forced Pedro to step down on April 7, 1831 and he left for Portugal leaving behind his five year old son, Pedro II. Until Pedro II was crowned in 1840, the country was ruled by regents and was marked by many local revolts. Pedro II's reign was highlighted by substantial rise in coffee exports, the War of the Triple Alliance and the end of slave trade from Africa (Brazil stopped trading slaves from Africa in 1850 and stopped slavery altogether in 1888, becoming the last country to ban slavery in America). By 1870's the Emperor's control on domestic politics began to fall. Finally the empire fell to a military coup. By 1889, Pedro II had stepped down and the Republican system had been adopted in Brazil. General Deodoro da Foneseca became the first de facto President through military ascension. The country's name became the Republic of the United States of Brazil (in 1967, it was changed to Federative Republic of Brazil). Between the years 1889 and 1930, the states of Sao Paulo and Minas Gerais alternated control of the nation.

In 1930, a military junta took control of the country. Getulio Vargas became the dictatorial ruler until 1945. He was reelected in 1951 and remained in office until his suicide in 1954. Juscelino Kubitschek's office years (1956-1961) was marked by the motto "50 anos em 5" (fifty years of development in five years). The military forces again took control of the country in 1964 and remained in force until 1985 when it fell due to political differences. Jose Sarney was sworn in as the President. Democracy was restored in 1988 when the Federal Constitution was enacted. Fernando Collor de Mello was the first truly elected President after the military regime. However in 1992 the President was impeached and the vice president Itamar Franco assumed the presidency. Itamar Franco's administration implemented the Plano Real economic package. This included introducing a new temporarily pegged currency the Real to the US dollar. The then finance minister Fernando Henrique Cardoso became the President in 1994 and was also reelected in 1998. The current President is Luiz Inacio Lula de Silva elected in 2002 and reelected in 2006.

1.2 GOVERNMENT AND POLITICS

The Brazilian Federation is based on three autonomous political entities-the State, Municipalities and the Federal District. The three entities are independent and harmonious among themselves, are the powers of the Union. The Federation is based on six fundamental principles-the sovereignty, citizenship, dignity of the people, social value of labour, freedom of enterprise and political pluralism. The division of power encompasses the Executive, the Legislative and the Judiciary branches, formally established by the Constitution. The Executive and Legislatives are organized independently at all four levels of political entities, and all members of the Executive and Legislative branches are elected by direct suffrage. Voting is compulsory for all citizens above the age of 18 years. The Judiciary is organized only at the Federal and state levels and the judges and other authorities are appointed after they clear the entry exam.

Four political parties stand out among the several small ones: Workers' Party (PT), Brazilian Social Democratic Party (PSDB), Brazilian Democratic Movement Party (PMDB) and Democrats (formally Liberal Front Party-PFL). The government is democratic republican and is of the Presidential form. The President is the Head of State and Head of Government, elected for a four-year term with a possibility of a second term. The President appoints the Ministers of State who helps him in governing the country. The National Congress is the Federation's bicameral legislature, comprising of the Chamber of Deputies (the lower house of National Congress, currently consisting of 513 deputies who are elected by proportional representation to serve four year terms) and the Federal Senate (the upper house of the National Congress, consisting of 81 seats-three from each state and three from the federal district to serve eight year terms). Elections are staggered so that two-third of the house is elected at a time while the remaining one-third after four years.

1.3 ECONOMY

Brazil has a diversified middle-income economy with variations in development levels. According to the International Monetary Fund and the World Bank, Brazil is the ninth largest economy in the world in terms of Purchasing Power Parity and the tenth largest in market exchange rates. Brazil's GDP is the highest in Latin America and has a developed agricultural, mining, manufacturing and services sectors. Major exports of the country include aircraft, coffee, automobiles, soybean, steel, ethanol, textiles, footwear and electronic equipments. Most large industry is located in the Southern and South East states. The Northeast is the poorest region of Brazil but the region is also attracting new investments in infrastructure for tourism sector and intensive agricultural schemes.

Brazil had pegged its currency, the real, to the U.S. dollar in 1994. However since the East Asian financial crisis, the Central Bank had temporarily changed its monetary policy to a managed-float scheme, until definitely changing the exchange regime to free-float in January 1999. Brazil received an IMF rescue package in 2002 amounting to US$ 30.4 billion, a record sum at the time. The loan was paid off early in 2005 by the Central Bank (due date was in 2006)

1.3.1 Population

According to the Census in the year 2000, the population of Brazil is 169,799,170 with a density of 22 per sq. km. In 2003, the adult literacy rate was at 88.6% of the population and the youth literacy rate (15 to 19 yrs) was 93.4%. The Human Development Index for Brazil ranks it the 70th country of the world (high index of 0.8). The Human Poverty Index of 9.7 ranks Brazil as 23rd rank out of the 108 developing countries.

The new Constitution reserves 25% of state and municipal taxes and 18% of federal taxes for education. Private school programs are available to complement the public school system. In 2003, the literacy rate was at 88 % of the population, and the youth literacy rate (ages 15–19) was 93.2 %. However, according to UNESCO Brazil's education still shows very low levels of efficiency by 15-year-old students, particularly in the public school network.

1.4 SECTORAL GROWTH

From Portugal's discovery of Brazil in 1500 to 1930, Brazil was subject to imperial mercantile policy that seriously restricted the development of the country. During this period the country relied mainly on production of primary products for exports. The colonial period left long lasting effects on the social and economic development of Brazil. Changes began to occur only in the late 18th century, when slavery was abolished and wage labour was adopted. The first step towards a change to modern industralised Brazil began only in 1930. The period of 1950 to 1980 witnessed high growth rates and the establishing of a diversified manufacturing base. However in the early 1980's, the country went through a period of extreme difficulties of slow growth and stagnation.

Socioeconomic transformation took place rapidly after World War II. In the 1940s, only 31.3 % of Brazil's 41.2 million inhabitants resided in towns and cities; by 1991, of the country's 146.9 million inhabitants 75.5 % lived in cities, and Brazil had two of the world's largest metropolitan centers—São Paulo and Rio de Janeiro. The rate of population growth decreased from about 3% annually in the 1950s and 1960s to 1.9 % annually in the 1980-91 period, indicating that Brazil was in a demographic transition. In the 2007 estimate, the rate of growth of population was 1.008%. 20% of the population was engaged in agricultural activities in 2003. Industries absorbed 14% while services remained the main employer with 66% of population engaged in it.

Primary sector comprises of agriculture, forestry and fishing. The secondary sector includes mostly manufacturing activities while the tertiary sector has the commerce, finance, transport and services activities. The share of the primary sector in the gross national product declined from 28 % in 1947 to 11 % in 1992. This further reduced to 5.1% in the 2007 estimate. Despite this reduction, the agricultural sector remains important. Although part of it is primitive and intensive, part is modern and dynamic. Brazil remains one of the world's largest exporters of agricultural products.

In the same 1947-92 period, the contribution of industry to GNP increased from less than 20 % to 39 %. The 2007 estimate puts the contribution of industries at 30.8% of GDP. The industrial sector produces a wide range of products for the domestic market and for export, including consumer goods, intermediate goods, and capital goods. By the early 1990s, Brazil was producing about 1 million motor vehicles annually and about 32,000 units of motor-driven farming machines. On an annual basis, it was also producing 1.8 million tons of fertilizers, 4.7 million tons of cardboard and paper, 20 million tons of steel, 26 million tons of cement, 3.5 million television sets, and 3 million refrigerators. In addition, about 70 million cubic meters of petroleum were being processed annually into fuels, lubricants, propane gas, and a wide range of petrochemicals. Furthermore, Brazil has at least 161,500 kilometers of paved roads and more than 63 million megawatts of installed electric power capacity. In 2005, the electricity output was 396.4 billion kWh.

1.4.1 Agriculture

Agricultural development in Brazil can be classified into two distinct periods: the horizontal expansion (from 1949 to 1969); and conservative modernization, (from 1970 to the present.) In the postwar years, Brazilian agriculture included an export sector that depended mainly on coffee. Other exports include cotton, sugar, and a few minor commodities. The country's population, its per capita income, and its urban sector had not yet started to impose a large demand on the agricultural sector. The situation however changed when the government imposed Import-Substitution Strategy for Industrialization. The strategy relied a lot on agricultural sector. It required that the agricultural sector generate most of the economy's foreign exchange, produce growing outputs of food and some industrial inputs, and transfer resources for import-substitution industrialization. The transfer mechanism was a tax on the foreign exchange earned by coffee exports and the persistent implicit taxation of agriculture. However the strategy resulted in an overvalued currency, the cruzeiro leading to the virtual exclusion of many agricultural products from the world market. Consequently, the cheap domestic food policy that prevailed depressed prices in favor of the urban-industrial sector.

In spite of the problems faced by the sector, the overall performance of agriculture during the horizontal expansion period was adequate. Agricultural GDP increased 4.2 % a year between 1949 and 1969, a considerably higher growth rate than that of the population; between 1950 and 1959, food production increased 5.4% a year, and the production of exportables rose 4.1% annually. The incorporation of new land in the expansion phase, especially along the agricultural frontier was made possible by an aggressive policy of road construction. Moreover, the disincentives of the import-substitution industrialization policies were overcome by maintaining ample access to land at concessionary terms.

By the late 1960s, the horizontal growth of agriculture was reaching its limits rapidly and it became clear that an increase in productivity was required for a continued expansion of production. The growth strategy of the military regime also required a fast expansion of exports, including agricultural commodities. Thus, the government implemented a conservative modernization strategy consisting of technical change for a restricted number of sub-sectors and incentives for the formation of agribusiness complexes.

Technical change in agriculture involved the development and adaptation of green-revolution technologies that was mainly concentrated on large agricultural operations that had important roles for mechanization and chemical inputs. Regarding the agribusiness complexes, the government provided strong incentives for the creation and expansion of processing industries and for the development and modernization of agricultural input industries. Certain products such as the soy meal and oil, instant coffee, processed beef, poultry, orange juice, and sugar and alcohol agribusiness complexes received many benefits like subsidized credit, guaranteed prices, tax exemptions and subsidies when exported. Traditional, unprocessed, agricultural products, however, were subjected to heavy taxation and to price and other controls. Consequently, products benefiting from agricultural modernization responded well to the conservative modernization strategy. Their production methods underwent considerable technical change, and their production and yields increased markedly. Traditional products, however, failed to modernize and tended to perform poorly. They were frequently subjected to price controls, export restrictions and quotas, and also to competition from subsidized imports when they failed to supply the domestic market adequately.

Crop production between 1970 and 1990 show that the components of the modern segment grew considerably, both in production and in yield, while those of the traditional segment stagnated or declined. At the beginning of the 1990s, the main crops in the modern segment were cocoa, cotton, rice, sugarcane, oranges, corn, soybeans, and wheat; those in the traditional segment included beans, manioc (cassava), bananas, peanuts, and coffee.

Brazil is also one of the largest exporters of guavas, lemons, mangoes, passion fruit, tangerines, and tobacco. The growth in export crops allowed Brazil to become one of the world's largest soybean producers and to earn needed foreign exchange. It also allowed the substitution of sugarcane alcohol for imported oil.

In 2003, 20 % of Brazil's economically active population worked in agriculture, down from 23.3% in 1990. Total arable and permanent crop area comprises 65.3 million hectares (161 million acres). Although agriculture's share of exports has declined relative to industrial goods, the value has continued to increase, so that Brazil in 1977 became the world's second-largest exporter of agricultural products. Except for grain (particularly wheat), of which some 7 million tons had to be imported in 2001, Brazil is virtually self-sufficient in food. The growth rates for agriculture as a whole averaged 2.8% during_1980–1990, and 3.2% for 1990–2000. By 1999, agricultural production was 20.2% higher than during 1989–91. In 2000, agricultural contribution was 7%, which reduced to 5% in 2007. Export crops are significant—in addition to the traditional exports of coffee and cocoa, Brazil is also a major exporter of soybeans and orange juice. In 1999, Brazil ranked fourth in the production of cocoa beans (after Côte d'Ivoire, Ghana, and Indonesia) at 206,000 tons, or 7.1% of the world's cocoa bean production. In recent years, however, the effects of the witches-broom fungus have devastated production.[1]

Coffee, until 1974 expereminent among export earners, has been declining in importance since the early 1960s, while soybeans, sugarcane, cotton, wheat, and citrus fruits have shown dramatic increases. Brazil led the world in coffee production in 2002/2003, at 3,096,000 tons. Sugarcane production, in which Brazil ranked first in the world in 2002/2003, is grown not only for refined sugar but also as a source of alcohol for fuel, and totaled 22,750,000 tons that season. In 1999, production included 22,772,000 tons of oranges, 20,973,000 tons of cassava, and 125,000 tons of cashews. Tobacco production in 2002 totaled 570,150 tons, 10% of world

1 Encyclopedia of the Nations...Brazil

production. Agricultural production in 2000/2001 (in millions of tons) was corn, 35.5; soybeans, 39.0; rice, 6.9; wheat, 3.3; and cottonseed, 1.5. Further agricultural reforms have been carried out under the Carta de Brasília of 1967. The Carta included an incentive program for the construction of storage facilities, to permit farmers to hold products off the market in expectation of better prices. Agricultural research in Brazil is conducted by the Agriculture and Cattle Raising Institute of Research. The expansion of power, transportation, and communications systems during the 1970s further contributed to agricultural development.

1.4.2 Industry

Major industries of Brazil include iron and steel production, automobile assembly, petroleum processing, chemicals production, and cement making. Technologically based industries have been the most dynamic in recent years, but have not been able to outpace the traditional industries. Peak industrial growth was achieved in 1973, when the manufacturing sector grew by 15.8%; growth rates averaging about 7% were posted during 1978–80, rising to 8.3% in 1985 and 11.3% in 1986. Growth slowed significantly during the 1990s. According to the Brazilian Statistical Institute (IBGE), manufacturing increased at an annual average of only 0.7% between 1988 and 1998. Manufacturing expanded from 2.6% growth in the third quarter of 2002 to 6.6% in the fourth quarter. Growth in 2002 was particularly pronounced in the construction industry.

In the Iron and Steel industries, in 1969, 3.7 million tons of crude steel was produced; by 1985, this had reached 20.5 million tons; and by 1998 the total output of processed ore was 190 million tons. Domestic production exceeds domestic needs. Vast reserves of accessible, high-grade ore, along with a rapidly expanding domestic demand for these products, helped in the continued expansion of the steel industry. Companhia Vale do Rio Doce (CVRD) is the largest Brazilian mining company, responsible for nearly 23% of the mineral output of the country.

Considered to be the industrial backbone of Brazil, motor vehicle production experienced a drop of nearly 27% from 1998 to

1999 because of the country's financial difficulties. Production of automobiles went from about two million units in 1997, down to 1.6 million units in 1998. In 2001, Brazil produced 1,798,472 automobiles, an increase of 7% over 2000. In 2000, the country produced 70,304 heavy trucks, an increase of 27% over 1999. The automobile industry is expanding rapidly with major sources of foreign investment and the construction of new manufacturing plants.

Oil been an important natural resource of energy, Brazil mines and refines petroleum products. The country in 2002 had 13 oil refineries with a total production capacity of 1,786,000 barrels per day. According to 2006 estimates, the oil production of the country is approximately 1.59 million barrels per day. Because of increased domestic refining capacity during the 1970s, imports of petroleum products were less needed, and by 1979, Brazil was a net exporter of petroleum derivatives. In 1998, Brazil only imported 50% of its petroleum. It has been estimated that in January 2006 there were 11.6 billion barrels of oil reserves in Brazil.

Brazil's petrochemical industry emphasizes the production of synthetic rubber at Petrobrás' synthetic rubber plant. There are also over 500 pharmaceutical laboratories and plants in Brazil, the majority in São Paulo. Over 80% of the industry is foreign-owned. Increased construction demands boosted Brazil's cement production during the 1980s and 1990s. Brazil's electrical equipment industry manufactures computers, television sets, transistor radios, refrigerators, air conditioners, and many other appliances. Brazil has the largest textile industry in South America in terms of installed capacity and output, with nearly half of the spindles and looms in operation on the continent. The Brazilian pulp and paper sector is also large, consisting of more than 220 companies, which together employ approximately 80,000 people in industrial operations, as well as another 57,000 in forestry work and operations. The pulp and paper sector is almost fully privately owned. The government allowed foreign investment in vital industries since 1995, and supports the sale of any residual parastatal enterprises.

1.4.3 Financial institutions

A banking reform enacted in December 1964 established the Central Bank of the Republic of Brazil (in 1967, became the Central Bank of Brazil) and was given powers to regulate the banking sector and the stock market. The reform also created the National Monetary Council that formulates the monetary policies for the Central Bank.

There once were about 340 commercial banks in Brazil, with hundreds of branch offices; however, banking reforms reduced that number to 233 in 1998. The largest banks are the federal banks Bank of Brazil, the Federal Savings Bank, and Brazilian Development Bank (BNDES); private banks Bradesco, Itau, Unibanco, Safra, and Banespa; the Real Bank, and the state bank of Rio Grande do Sul, Banrisul. The Bank of Brazil primarily finances projects in the agricultural sector. The BNDES provide long-term financing and administers the privatization program.

Since January 1994, banks and other financial institutions must publish constant-currency financial statements. The major banks are considered to be sophisticated and competitive, many operating on-line, and offer a broad range of financial services.

1.4.4 Foreign Direct Investment

FDI began to gain importance in Brazil in the late 19th century, especially through the British investments in services related to export activities such as railroads, sea roads etc. In case of manufacturing sector, FDI gained prominence only after the Second World War. Reductions in economy's anti-export bias in the late 1960's lead the transnational corporations in to deeper involvement with foreign trade via exports. These companies contributed greatly to Brazil's diversification of exports right through the 1970's.

The crisis of 1980's practically wiped out Brazil from the FDI map. On an average the annual net inflow of FDI to the country decreased from US$ 2.3 billion in 1971-81 to just about US$ 357 million between 1982 and 1991. The 1990's marked the revival of Brazil as a relevant destination for FDI. Between 1990 and 1995,

Brazil received about US$ 2 billion a year in FDI. Until the mid 1990's the FDI was concentrated in capital and technology intensive industries, at the end of the decade the stock of FDI was far from diversified: services gained prominence and there was more participation of industrial sectors intensive in natural resources, including mining sectors (oil and gas), the countries of origin have also diversified although United States remained the main country. This became possible due to the Constitutional amendments in 1995 that opened formerly closed sectors such as petroleum, telecommunications, mining, power generation and internal transport to foreign investors.

In 2000, the figure touched $32.8 billion. Then onward, the flow decreased. Even then, the inflows in 2001 amounted to 21 billion, 3% of the world's total. In 2003, the flow of FDI's to Brazil suffered a sharp reduction falling to just US$ 10.1 billion, 45% lower than 2002.

Foreign direct investment flows into Brazil rose 80% in 2004, to reach more than US$18 billion, according to a report by the Economic Commission for Latin America and the Caribbean (**ECLAC**). Brazil received more FDI than any country in the region. For Brazil this could be a unique opportunity to consolidate a new, higher quality investment cycle, according to **ECLAC**. The country seems to have recovered its leading role as a receiver of FDI from transnational companies, lost after the wave of macroeconomic instability that it experienced in 1999 and 2000. Brazil is one of the economies with the most transnational companies in the world: 400 of the companies on the Fortune 500 list still have a presence in the country.

Brazil's participation as a foreign investor is negligible. Nevertheless some factors such as the Mersour integration induced some nationally owned firms to move internationally. The 1990's witnessed Argentina as a destination of FDI from Brazilian companies. Since 1990's the outflow of FDI from Brazil have been increasing occasionally, with heavy fluctuations in the recent years. Brazil is the most important source of FDI from the Latin American countries in 2002 with outflow of $ 2.5 billion.

In 2004, the main destination sectors for FDI were the food and beverage industry, led by the merger between *AmBev* and the Belgian *Interbrew*, and telecommunications, in which the Mexican firm *Telmex* bought the fixed telephone company, *Embratel*. At the retail level, *Wal Mart* (United States) bought the *Bompreço* supermarket chain, and in the energy sector, the main operation was a capital increase by *Endesa* (Spain) for one of its subsidiaries.

The investment boom of the 1990s was driven by economic stabilization, the programme to privatize state companies, the elimination of restrictions on foreign capital, and the creation of Mercosur, along with sectoral incentives. In contrast, the current cycle is characterized by the purchase of private firms. The main reason motivating the transnational corporations seems to be the same in both cases: the search for new markets.

FDI has recently regained some ground in the manufacturing sector and has partially reversed its anti-export bias. The contraction of the domestic market in 2001-2003 and the gains in competitiveness brought about by the devaluation have prompted companies to adopt efficiency-seeking strategies aimed at conquering new markets. These new strategies serve to complement these firms' traditional strategies for expanding their domestic market share. This shift has been occurring in both the electronics and the automobile industries.

Brazil has become a true laboratory for the changes taking place in the world car industry. Important vehicle assembly firms, such as the German firm, *Volkswagen*, the American *General Motors* and *Ford*, and the French company *Peugeot-Citroën (PSA)* have built modular plants to develop new, more competitive models.

In its report, **ECLAC** argues that this is an opportunity for Brazil to capture new kinds of FDI and improve its international competitiveness. It recommends developing a policy that involves reducing factors called the "Brazil cost": the tax burden, deficient infrastructure, and regulatory problems. Moreover, it suggest creating new policies for investment and to strengthen a body for attracting investment that identifies the best opportunities and evaluate impacts in the context of national development goals.

1.4.5 Energy Policy

After nearly three decades of work, Brazil has successfully developed a cost-effective alternative to gasoline. Along with new offshore oil discoveries, that's a big reason Brazil expects to become energy independent.

The first oil shock in 1973, sparked by an oil embargo amid war in the Middle East, quadrupled the price of oil. Few places were hit harder than Brazil, which imported 80% of its fuel at the time. Within months, the economy slid into recession. About 40% of its foreign-exchange income was used to import oil.

In 1975, Brazil's military leader, Gen. Ernesto Geisel, ordered that the country's gasoline supply be mixed with 10% ethanol, a level Brazil steadily raised to 25% over the next five years. That meant the same amount of gasoline would last longer. It also allowed Brazil to pay for fuel with local currency, in the form of payments to farmers.

To help the nascent industry, the government gave sugar companies cut-rate loans to build ethanol plants and guaranteed prices for their product. The government also funded Urbano Ernesto Stumpf, an ethanol researcher at a Brazilian Air Force laboratory, who was developing a car that would run on ethanol alone.

In November 1976, three ethanol-powered cars created by Mr. Stumpf — a Beetle, a Dodge and a Brazilian car called a Gurgel — embarked on a 5,000 mile trip aimed to demonstrate to Brazilians that ethanol really worked. The São Paulo state telephone company converted 400 gasoline cars into ethanol ones displaying the logo: "Powered by Alcohol."

After the 1979 Iranian revolution caused the world's second oil-price shock, Brazil sped up its efforts, initiating what became known as the Proalcool program. Brazil's new leader, Gen. Joao Baptista Figueiredo, ordered sugar companies to ramp up production. He also required state-run oil giant Petrobras to make the fuel available at filling stations. Car companies received tax breaks to get ethanol-powered vehicles into showrooms. By the end of the year, Italian car maker Fiat SpA was offering an ethanol-only car for sale. Within a year, every foreign and domestic auto company in Brazil had followed suit.

While motorists grew fond of the made-in-Brazil fuel, there was a cost in the form of hefty government subsidies. Consulting firm Datagro, which counts Brazil's biggest sugar companies as its clients, estimates that Brazil spent at least $16 billion in 2005 dollars from 1979 to the mid-1990s on loans to sugar companies and price supports. The Datagro estimate doesn't include foregone revenue from tax breaks as well as other costs to consumers.

At current prices, Brazil can make ethanol for about $1 a gallon, according to the World Bank. That compares with the international price of gasoline of about $1.50 a gallon. Even though ethanol gets less mileage than gasoline, in Brazil it's still cheaper per mile driven. As a result, ethanol now accounts for as much as 20% of Brazil's transport fuel market. The country's use of gasoline has actually declined since the late 1970s. The use of alternative fuels in the rest of the world is a scant 1%.

With government support, sugar companies and auto makers' local units delivered cost-saving breakthroughs. "Flexible fuel" cars running ethanol, gasoline or a mixture of both, have become a hit. Car buyers no longer have to worry about fluctuating prices for either fuel because flex-fuel cars allow them to hedge their bets at the pump. Seven out of every 10 new cars sold in Brazil are flex-fuel.

Brazil is also fortunate that sugar is the cheapest way to make ethanol and Brazil has the right conditions for growing the crop — plenty of land, rain and cheap labor.

Despite these unique circumstances, Brazil's efforts are being closely followed by countries with big fuel bills. India and China have sent top officials to see Brazil's program. India, the world's second-biggest sugar producer behind Brazil, mandated in 2003 that nine of its states add a 5% ethanol mixture to gas. The Brazilian unit of Germany's Volkswagen AG, the first car maker to introduce a flex-fuel model in Brazil, has received 38 delegations from more than a dozen countries in the past year alone, VW officials say.

Brazil says its ethanol exports will likely double to $1.3 billion in 2010 from $600 million in 2005, largely to Japan and Sweden. These countries hope using ethanol — which releases less carbon dioxide than fossil fuels — will help them meet their obligations under the Kyoto Protocol to cut emissions.

1.5 EMERGING TECHNOLOGIES IN BRAZIL

1.5.1 Genetic Technology

In Brazil, the agricultural sector is using genetically modified seeds to increase production of crops such as soybean. Non-government organizations however prevented the farmers from using the technology from September 1998 to December 2003. During this period however GM soybean was cultivated illegally and looking at the land under the crops, 1/3 of soy area is under the GM variety. Another important problem of the loss of topsoil was solved due to the discovery of a gene that lets plants tolerate glyph sate (an herbicide) and transferring it to the crop. Another advantage is that the plant residues of the crops do not get oxidized when ploughing exposes them to air. Carbon dioxide, a greenhouse gas is therefore not produced. Global warming thus gets reduced.

It is an accepted fact that in order to reap the benefits of the genetic revolution the agricultural sector needs to be organized. Brazil tripled its grain production in the last four decades, but it was a long-term plan. In anticipation of the gene revolution in the seventies, Brazil has been making consistent investment in training human resources in fields of plant cell, molecular and development biology.

In 2007, Brazil retained its position as the third largest adopter of biotech crops in the world, estimated at 15.0 million hectares, of which 14.5 million hectares were planted with RR® soybean and 500,000 hectares planted with a single gene Bt cotton, grown for the second time in 2007. Considering both percentage and absolute growth, the year-over-year growth of 30% between 2006

(11.5 million hectares) and 2007 (15.0 million hectares) was the second highest in the world after India; the increase of 3.5 million hectares in 2007 was the largest absolute increase for any biotech crop country in the world. Brazil is currently the second largest producer of soybeans in the world after the USA and expected to become the first in the future – in 2007; Brazil offset a reduction in biotech soybean hectarage in the USA. Brazil is the third largest producer of maize in the world and the first biotech maize varieties have received initial clearance and are expected to have final approval for planting in 2008/09. Brazil is also the sixth largest producer of cotton, the tenth largest grower of rice (3.7 million hectares) and the only major producer of rice outside Asia. In addition, Brazil is also the largest sugarcane producer in the world with 6.2 million hectares and uses approximately half of its national sugarcane area to produce sugar and the other half for the production of ethanol for biofuels. After the USA, Brazil was the second biggest producer of ethanol in the world in 2007 and one of few countries that is self-sufficient in both fossil fuels and biofuels in which it is a world leader. To date, the introduction of biotech crops in Brazil has suffered significant delays because of legal and judicial restraining orders delaying the deployment of approved biotech crops. A 2007 study by Dr. Anderson Galvão Gomes, has estimated the benefits lost to Brazilian farmers because of delayed approval due to a cumbersome approval process, particularly the legal challenges from various interest groups, including Ministries within the Government. Taking the fast adoption rates of RR® soybean in neighboring Argentina as a practical bench mark for adoption, the study concluded that delayed approval of RR® soybean in Brazil for the period 1998 to 2006 cost farmers US$3.10 billion and cost technology developers an additional US$1.41 billion, for a total of US$4.51 billion in lost benefits. The total potential benefits for both farmers and technology developers during the period 1998 to 2006 was US$6.6 billion of which only US$2.09 billion, equivalent to 31%, was realized. Thus, US$4.51 billion was lost due to legal delays which were a significant sacrifice for Brazil as a nation and the major losers were farmers. However, recent commitments by the current administration of funds totaling Real 10 billion equivalent to US$7 billion (60% public and 40% private), and prorated at US$700 million per year for the next ten years, demonstrates strong political will and support for biotechnology by the Brazilian government. Moreover, a significant part of the US$7 billion is to be devoted to biofuels and agriculture. In November 2007 President Luis Inacio Lula da Silva of Brazil announced a US$23 billion investment in a four-year "Plan for Action for Science, Technology and Innovation." One of the four thrusts of the Plan is to support research and innovation in strategic areas particularly biotechnology, biofuels and biodiversity. It is noteworthy that the political will for biotechnology evident in Brazil is also evident in China and India. The troika of Brazil, India and China is a formidable force in agricultural biotechnology that can deliver enormous material and humanitarian benefits. The political will of the troika needs to be integrated to establish a nuclear group that will work together to gain the support of global society for harnessing and optimizing the contribution of biotech crops for the alleviation of poverty and hunger for resource-poor farmers by 2015 – the Millennium Development Goals – when it is expected that all three major staples, maize, rice and wheat as well as several orphan crops will benefit from biotechnology. In summary, Brazil has become a world leader in the adoption of biotech crops with continued significant growth expected in RR® soybean hectarage, rapid expansion in Bt cotton supplemented with herbicide tolerance, substantial opportunities on the 13 million hectares of maize from 2008 onwards, new opportunities for its 3.7 million hectares of rice, as well as the enormous potential with biotech sugarcane for its emerging role as a world leader and exporter of bioethanol.

Brazil has new biosafety laws that came to force on March 24, 2005. According to these laws the National Biosafety Council takes the final decisions on commercialization of GM products. The law also legalizes the production and marketing of transgenic glyphosate-resistant soybean, and planting of saved seed in 2004/05. CNTBio announced the approval of the sale of the Bollgard Bt cottonseed in Brazil on 18 March 2005. The decision was based on two conditions. Zones of exclusion must first be established in some parts of Brazil where Bt cotton may not be planted at all to protect the natural population of other species and races. Secondly 20% of the cotton area must be a refuge area of conventional cotton at less than 800m from the transgenic crop. CTNBio has also requested a mitigation plan from Monsanto with good agricultural practices such as destruction of crop residues, crop rotation, use of trap crops and biological control.

The most contentious application of Genetic engineering is its use in humans- Cloning. A Clone is a copy of a plant, animal, microorganism or gene derived from a single common ancestor gene. The possibility of human cloning came when Scottish scientist at the Roslin Institute created the sheep "dolly" in 1996. The governments of many countries have banned the cloning and genetic modification of human beings. This technology is not allowed in Brazil even for therapeutic purposes-the Bio-safety Bill that is waiting for the approval by the country senate before becoming a law, has revoked strong responses from the scientific community. The most controversial item in the bill is the prohibition of research in embryonic stem cells, including that used in treating human diseases. The influential catholic and protestant churches of the country are promoting the bill. On May 28th 2008, the Brazilian Supreme Court ruled that scientists could conduct embryonic stem cell research. Advocates have said that this ruling could make Brazil Latin America's leader in Stem Cell Research. It holds promises of curing Parkinson's disease and diabetes. However the Court's ruling also raises ethical concerns about limits on human life. Brazil is the world's largest Roman Catholic country and the Church has condemned the embryonic research saying that life begins at conception and by destroying an embryo, scientists destroy human life. The Church leaders say they support adult stem cell research, which they consider ethically acceptable.

Considering the interdependence between agriculture and biodiversity, Brazil has made significant development in biotechnology mainly due to the Brazilian Agricultural Research

Corporation (EMBRAPA). Examples of such progress obtained by the Brazilian agricultural research system includes:

- Brazilian researchers have begun a study of wild rice populations in the Amazon region, which may lead to the identification of the genes responsible for resistance to disease and environmental stress.
- The results obtained by Embrapa in relation to nitrogen fixation in varieties of soybeans and other leguminous plants have resulted in savings in the use of fertilizers to the order of hundreds of millions of dollars a year.
- A project for the identification in maize germplasm collections of varieties and strains with genes and heterosis of importance to agronomy, with special reference to resistance to the main diseases of maize. This project emphasizes the importance of tropical germplasm in enhancement programmes.
- Research on the control of diseases of oranges caused by bacteria (citric canker, chlorosis). This programme is of special significance considering that Brazil is the world's largest exporter of concentrated orange juice.
- Studies to combine improvement with the characterisation of the molecular structure of germplasm, to increase the resistance of cattle to diseases and increase productivity.
- Mapping of the sugar cane genome, and the development of biodegradable plastics from sugar cane.
- Techniques for propagation by cloning and programs of genetic improvement of eucalyptus have facilitated considerable expansion in the paper and pulp industry, promoting the use of plantations and reducing dependence on native forests.
- Some projects are being carried out which involve the production of genetically modified organisms (GMO), for example, the production of virus resistant potatoes, and herbicide-resistant beans, soybeans and sugar cane.

- In addition to these projects, several new species of maize, cotton and soybean, genetically modified with the *Bacilus thuringannsis* (Bt) gene for resistance to insects, which have been produced by private international companies, are being tested on a small scale. They have been approved be the National Technical Commission for Biosafety (Comissão Técnica Nacional de Biossegurança – CTNBio) of the Ministry of Science and Technology – MCT.

1.5.2 Robotics and Artificial Intelligence

The International Robotics and Artificial Intelligence Fair held in Brazil aims to promote robotics in industries as well as to attract students and promote the study of science and technology in the nation. Robots are widely used in the field of medicine. Miguel Nicolelio the renowned Brazilian neurosurgeon has introduced the world first operation on the human brain that will allow the brain to control the robotic arm. The experiment opened the way for the creation of robots that can be controlled by the force of the mind.

The International Robotics and Artificial Intelligence Fair held in Brazil, 2007 has two main objectives- to show the industry that robotics are more accessible and necessary and secondly, to attract students and stimulate the people's curiosity to promote science and technology in Brazil. According to the Director of the event, Eduardo Branco it is the age of Robotic Revolution- in the industry, medicine and in every day life. The main aim is to awaken Brazilians to this new reality. The Fair introduced many new robots to the industry such as the KR16 robot that will make a miniature automobile during the event. In order to stimulate the students other robots such as the Scara robot that will play a game of checkers against the KR5 robot; the Robocar- a car that transforms into a six meter tall robot and so on, was also introduced.

1.5.3 Information Technology

The information policy in Brazil began in the late 1960's and early 1970's as an effort to develop a Brazilian personal computer.

Technology was to be transferred to a state owned corporation and to private firms owned by Brazilians. With the development of the personal computers, a policy was devised that restricted the new market to Brazilian firms but allowed the presence of multinational companies in the area of mainframe computers. There was a strict ban for seven years on the import of microcomputers. The protectionist attitude was very controversial and drew strong opposition from United State Government on the basis of free trade.

Brazil has also introduced Artificial Intelligence in Consumer Rights Protection. In the early 1990's the Brazilian government introduced legislation to update consumer protection laws and regulations. Inspite of the new step, consumer protection still lacks efficiency. In order to solve the problem researchers along with many government agencies developed the Santa Catarina Consumer Portal to offer consumers unprecedented protection and strengthen market confidence. The agencies plan to create a model for legal assistance in consumer rights issues. The project is a first proposal for Information Technology implementation and Artificial Intelligence techniques for e-governance. Consumer SC intends to globalise consumer assistance services and to spread knowledge over the entire country. It will be the first portal in the country to bring together scientific and academic research, e-government services, software and free virtual legal assistance in matters concerning consumer rights.

The Brazilian government has emphasized controlled privatisation and deregulation in order to provide the business sector with an environment in which it can grow and adapt quickly to the changing economic and business climate while at the same time still be subject to competition. In the early 1980's Brazil had imposed strict restrictions in order to promote its own domestic industries. This decade is referred to as the lost decade characterized by high inflation and economic stagnation. The lack of external finance and investment further lead the country to protectionism in order to keep a trade surplus. By the early1990's Brazil was far behind in the Information Age and decided to remove the strict tariffs. Since then Brazil has followed a policy of deregulation in order to enable the industry to catch up with the advancements in the field.

The term Digital Divide refers to the problem among developing countries where large sections of the population do not have access to technology. The most common examples are Internet, telephones, and computers. Brazil also faces this problem – there are large segments of the population that do not have electricity and telephones, mainly the northern and central section near the Amazon and mountain ranges. The country has a definite economic divide- the top 5% of the population control over 50% of the national economy. One of the measures taken by the government to narrow down this divide is the "popular PC project". Popular PC is a bare-bones personal computer that will help grant more access to underserved citizens. It has all the necessary hardware minus the storage capacity such as the floppy drive. Another programme is the "Computers for All" meant for low-income families above the poverty line. It consists of subsidizing lines of credit to buy computers and since its launch 77,000 machines have been marketed.

Another example of how technology can help makes lives easier for the visually impaired is the new soft ware by Microsoft. The technology introduced in Brazil is also used to create employment opportunities for the visually impaired in the software industry. The Micro Power's Virtual Vision is a typing programme adapted to home banking. The components read the screen of home banking via the Internet and transfer the information to a voice synthesizer. The contents of the page are then narrated to the user, who can then utilize services ranging from account balances to transferring funds and paying bills. It is the first commercial screen-reading software to support Portuguese, the national language of Brazil. Since the launch, about 500 Brandesco customers have installed the software to access their bank account and conduct the financial transactions through the Internet.

Until privatisation began in 1990's the telecommunication sector's authority was with the Ministry of Communication and the controlling agency were Telebras and the State Postal Company.

In 1997 the National Telecommunication Agency (ANATEL) was created to enable a new model for Brazil telecommunications with the main role of regulation, concession and supervision of its services in the country.

1.5.4 Nanotechnology

Brazil send her first astronaut in space on March 30th 2006 Lt. Col. Marcos Pontes to conduct nano-research in space. Although the exact nature of the research is not made known, it is believed that about nine nano-technology related experiments were conducted.

Various researches are been carried out in Brazil in the field of nanotechnology. After ten years of work wit the nanostructure systems, the Medical School of University of Sao Paulo (USP) created an incubator called Nanocore biotechnology. The research group first produced biodegradable nanoparticles in the shape of nanocapsules that contain the active ingredient of the drug or vaccine. This would be released only when the target has been reached –as in Chemotherapy. A partnership of UFRGS (Federal University of Rio Grande do Sul) and the oil company Petrobras' research center has led to the development of nanocatalyzers that remove the oil compounds that pollute the environment during the refining stages of petrol and benzene. A joint research project of the Brazilian Agricultural research Corporation with the University of Sao Paulo and the University of Pennsylvania has led to the development of an "electronic tongue". It is made from nanostructured conducting polymers, and the apparatus is used to test and analyze the different beverages such as different brands of mineral water, types of coffee, wines etc. The sensitivity of the "tongue" is ten thousand times greater than the human being. The Federal University of Goias and the Federal University of Rio de Janeiro have created nanomagnets used for cleaning up water after petrol spills.

Brazilian research in nanoscience and nanotechnology is carried out in decentralized research networks and so the exact figures are difficult to obtain due to multiple funding sources. The country has good infrastucture and qualified personnel and now needs to attract private investments in the sector to apply their technical know-how and make the sector more competitive. There are no specific regulations on R&D in the field of nanotechnology. Currently there are no Government bodies involved in the creation of laws or guides for conduct in this area. Currently the Congress is discussing a draft bill called Law for Technological Innovation, facilitating an interaction between universities and enterprises that would cover the field of Nano S&T.

1.6 LINKAGES

Goldman Sach predicts that Brazil will emerge as an economic superpower in the role of a supplier of raw materials. It is true that Brazil has tremendous natural resources –be it oil, minerals or forest to take advantage of. The emerging technologies lend a helping hand in the process of development. Brazil is self sufficient in food except in grains. The genetic engineering scientists have developed biotech crops to solve the problem of shortages. Currently the country is the third largest adopter of such crops. Brazil is also the largest sugar cane producer in the world. Half the production is diverted to ethanol production and the rest go for sugar processing.

The industrial backbone of the country is the motor vehicle production. After the oil shocks hit the country, an alternative was required. The answer was ethanol- a cost effective one. Brazil is thus the only country that is self sufficient in both biofuels and fossil fuels.

Brazil is making efforts to reduce the digital divide among its people. Services such as e-governance are offered to spread knowledge. Inspite of its wealth, the incidence of poverty and inequality remains high. The North and North East are the poorer regions. Over 40 million Brazilians live on less than $2 a day and nearly 20 million on less than $1 a day. ICT can be a useful instrument to bridge this gap. Agricultural production is becoming increasingly knowledge based and science intensive. New strategic research in genetics has emerged that can greatly affect the capacity to produce food and manage the resources. The extent of success of a new discovery depends on how soon it can be implemented. A well developed network of ICT would help a great deal in this regard.

Regarding robotics and artificial intelligence, Brazil has a well developed motor vehicle industry. Robotics and automation can help to increase productivity and further boost the economic growth of the country.

The emerging technologies can thus help Brazil become a world superpower not only as a supplier of raw materials but also as an industrial superpower.

2 RUSSIA

Capital	— Moscow
Area	— 17,075,200 sq. km
Population	— 140,702,096 (July 2008 estimate)
Average rate of growth of population	— –0.474 %
Currency	— Russian Ruble(RUB)
GDP(PPP)	— $ 2.097 trillion(2007)
GDP (per capita PPP)	— $ 14,800 (2007)
GDP real growth rate	— 8.1% (2007)
Agriculture as a share of GDP	— 4.7% (2007)
Exports	— $355.5 billion (2007)
Life Expectancy at birth	— 65.94 years (2008)

Infant mortality rate	— 10.81 deaths/1000 live birth (2008 rest.)
Literacy	— 99.4% (2004)
Human Development Index	— 0.802 rank 67th

Curving across the North Pole in a huge arc, Russia's area is about 17 million sq. kms making it the largest country in the world. It covers more than one-eighth of the Earth's land area occupying much of Eastern Europe and northern Asia. With 141 million people, Russia is the ninth largest nation in terms of population. However the density of population is only 9 persons per sq. km (22 persons per sq. mile) making it one of the most sparsely populated country of the world. The center of Russia's population and economic activity is the European sector. Vast tracts of land are virtually unoccupied such as Siberia and the Artic region.

Russia has the world's largest forest reserves second only to the Amazon Rainforest, called the "lungs of Europe" because of the carbon dioxide it absorbs. With access to three of the world's oceans-the Atlantic, the Artic and the Pacific Ocean-Russian fishing fleets is a major contributor to the world's fish supply. Russia has thousands of rivers and inland water bodies, the most prominent one being Lake Baikal. It is the worlds' deepest, purest and most capacious fresh water lake containing one fifth of world fresh water supply.

2.1 BRIEF HISTORY

The ancestors of modern Russians are the Slavic tribes. According to the earliest Russian chronicles, a Varangian named Rurik was elected ruler of Novgorod around the year 860; his successors moved south and extended to Kiev. In the 10th and 11th centuries this state of Kievan Rus became the largest and most prosperous in Europe.

The most powerful successor state was the Great Duchy of Moscow. After the downfall of Constantinople in1453, Moscow claimed succession to Eastern Roman empire. Ivan III (Ivan the

Great) consolidated the surrounding areas under Moscow's dominion and took the title "Grand Duke of all the Russians". In 1547, Ivan IV was officially crowned the first Tsar of Russia. During his reign, Russia was transformed into a multiethnic state. He promulgated a new code of laws, established the first Russian feudal representative body and introduced local self-management in the rural areas. However his reign was also marked by the long and unsuccessful Livonian War against the coalition of Poland, Lithuania and Sweden for the access to the Baltic coast and sea trade. The War, epidemics and poor harvests weakened the state. The death of Ivan's sons and the famine (1601-1603) lead to civil war and foreign intervention in the Time of Troubles in early 1600's. Under the Romanov dynasty and Peter I the Russian empire was officially founded and the new capital St. Petersburg was established. Catherine II (1762-1796) continued the efforts to establish Russia as one of the great powers of Europe. Napoleon's invasion failed miserably in Russia due to the Russian resistance combined with the harsh and bitter Russian winter. However the Napoleonic Wars brought to Russia the ideas of liberalism and attempts were made to curtail the Tsar's powers during the revolt of 1825. The revolt was suppressed and was followed by several decades of political repression.

The prevalence of serfdom and the conservative policies of Nicolas I hindered the development of Russia in the mid 19th century. His successor Alexander II enacted several reforms such as the abolition of serfdom in 1861. However many socio-economic conflicts rose during his reign and continued during the reign of his son Nicholas II. In January 1905, workers peacefully demonstrated for reforms in factory condition and were fired upon by troops, killing and wounding hundreds. This event called "Bloody Sunday" set the Russian Revolution of 1905 in motion. Although the army quickly put down the uprising, Nicholas II was forced to concede major reforms such as granting the freedoms of speech and assembly, legalization of political parties and the creation of an elected legislative assembly, the Duma.

Russia entered the World War I in aid of its ally Serbia, but the public distrust of the regime was deepened by the rising costs of war, casualties and corruption. This led to the outbreak of the Russian Revolution of 1917. Democratically elected councils called Soviets, organized workers and peasants throughout the country for the uprising. The February Revolution overthrew the monarchy, which was replaced by the Provisional Government. While initially receiving the support of the Soviets, the Provisional Government was unable to resolve many of the problems that had lead to the Revolution. The second revolution, called the October Revolution was lead by Vladimir Lenin overthrew the Government and created the world's first communist state.

2.1.1 The Soviet Union

Following the October Revolution a civil war broke out between the new regime (the moderate socialist parties and Mensheviks) and its opponents, the White movement (a loose confederation of counter revolutionary forces). The Bolsheviks instituted "War Communism" to requisite food for the army and the cities, resulting in mass starvation and peasant resistance. Russia had now been at war for seven years during which 16 million people lost their lives. The economy and the infrastructure were also devastated.

Following the victory in the Civil War the Russian Soviet Federative Socialist Republic together with three other soviet republics formed the Soviet Union on December 30, 1922. Russia contributed more than half the population of the Soviet Union. The Bolshevik introduced free universal health, education and social security benefits. Russia became the first country in the world to have full freedom of divorce and legalize abortion. After Lenin's death in 1924, Joseph Stalin consolidated power and became dictator.

Stalin launched a command economy, forced rapid industrialization of the largely rural economy and collectivization of agriculture. At the end of 1930's Stalin launched the Great Purges, an act of repression against millions of people who were suspected to be a threat to the party were executed or exiled to Serbia or Central Asia. On June 22, 1941 Nazi Germany invaded the Soviet Union, thus began the Great Patriotic War, as it became known in the USSR. It was the largest theatre of war in the history in terms of the number of soldiers, equipment and casualties. It was notorious for its ferocity, destruction and immense loss of lives. Although the Germans had considerable success early on, eventually the Soviet Union was victorious, with an estimated 27 million of her people killed accounting for half of all World War causalities. Even though the economy suffered massive destruction, Soviet Union emerged as an acknowledged superpower. Becoming the world's second nuclear weapons power, the Soviet Union established the Warsaw Pact alliance and entered into a struggle for global dominance with the United States, which became known as the Cold War.

Stalin's successor Nikita Khrushchev launched the world's first artificial satellite; Sputnik 1 and Yuri Gagarin became the first human being to orbit the earth. Following his ousting, another period of collective leadership ensued until Leonid Brezhnev established himself in the early 1970's. Brezhnev's rule oversaw economic stagnation and the Soviet invasion of Afghanistan.

The reformist Mikhail Gorbachev introduced landmark policies of *glasnost* (openness) and *perestroika* (restructuring) from 1985 onwards. The policies aimed at maximal publicity, openness and transparency in all the activities of the government institutions in the Soviet Union. It meant that the harsh restrictions on free speech and open political discourse become possible. However the reforms put in motion forces of change that threatened the Communist Party while provoking strong resentments among the conservatives. The last years of the Soviet Union were characterized by shortages of goods in the grocery stores huge budget deficits and explosive growth of money supply leading to inflation. In August 1991, an unsuccessful attempt against Gorbachev aimed at preserving Soviet Union instead lead to its collapse. In Russia, Boris Yeltsin came to power and declared the end of the communist rule. The USSR broke up into fifteen independent republic states and was officially dissolved in December 1991. Boris Yeltsin was elected president in June 1991, in the first direct presidential election in Russian history.

2.1.2 Russian Federation

After the disintegration of USSR, the Russian economy went through major crisis. The end of the Soviet Union for Russia meant facing the world without the buffer zone of the soviet republics that had protected and nurtured it in many ways since 1920's. The change required a complete reorganization of what had become a corrupt and inefficient Soviet system. In October 1991, Yeltsin announced radical market oriented reforms along the lines of "shock therapy" as recommended by the US and IMF. However the policy resulted in economic collapse, with GDP falling about 50% between 1990 and 1995. The early and mid 1990's was marked by extreme lawlessness and rise in organized crime. A constitutional crisis in 1993 pushed Russia to the brink of civil war. Yeltsin illegally dissolved the country's legislature; in response the legislators barricaded themselves inside the White House and the country witnessed the deadliest street war ever seen in Moscow since the October Revolution. With military support, Yeltsin besieged the parliament building and used tanks and artillery to eject the legislators.

On December 31, 1999 Boris Yeltsin resigned from the presidency, handing the post to newly appointed prime minister, Vladimir Putin, who won the 2000 elections. High oil prices and cheap Ruble along with increasing domestic demand, consumption and investments has helped the economy to grow for eight straight years, alleviating the standards of living and increasing Russia's clout on the world stage. Although many reforms made under Putin's rule have been criticized as undemocratic, his leadership has provided stability and progress and won him widespread popularity in Russia.

2.2 GOVERNMENT AND POLITICS

According to the Constitution adopted on December 12, 1993, Russia is a federation and a Presidential republic where the President is the Head of the State and the Prime Minister is the Head of the Government. The President is elected for a four-year term. The Ministers comprises of the premier, his deputies and other selected individuals; all are appointed by the president. There is no Vice President in Russian government. If the President dies in office, cannot operate due to ill health, is impeached or resigns, the Prime Minister serves as the acting President till a new one is elected or appointed by the Duma. The recently held presidential election on March 2, 2008 has unveiled a new President Dmitriy Medvedev who assumed office on 7 May 2008. The National Legislature is the Federal Assembly comprising of two chambers-the 450 member State Duma and the 176-member Federation Council. Constitutional justice is based on equality of all citizens; judges are independent and subject only to the law. Leading parties in Russia include United Russia, the Communist Party, the Liberal Democratic Party of Russia and Fair Russia.

The Russian federation is recognized as the continued legal personality of the former Soviet Union in international law. The country has assumed the USSR's permanent seat on the UN Security Council and other international organizations.

2.3 ECONOMY

Economic growth has been bolstered in Russia by the high oil prices, foreign investment, increased domestic consumption and political stability. In 2006, Russia ended the year with its eighth straight year of growth, averaging 6.7% annually since 1998 financial crisis. Russia's GDP in 2006 was $1.723 trillion, the eighth highest in the world. In 2007, Russia's GDP grew at 7.6%. About 12.5% of Russians were below the designated poverty line in 2007 thus showing a decline from 33.5% in 1992. About 4.6% of the people are engaged in the agricultural sector generating 10.8% of GDP, while the industrial sector engages 39.1% population and generates 28.8% income. The services sector employs 56.3% Russians and contributes 60.5% to the country's GDP.

More than 80% of Russian exports comprises of oil, natural gas, metals and timber. Russia has the world's largest reserves of natural gas and is the second largest exporter of the product. The country is also the world's second largest exporter of oil. The importance of oil and gas in the economy has lead to the creation of the Stabilising Fund of the Russian Federation. The Fund takes in the revenue from oil and gas to help offset the market volatility. As of October 1, 2007, it stands at $ 147.6 billion. Over the past few years, Russia has used her Stabilisation Fund to repay all Soviet-era debt to Paris Club creditors and the IMF. Oil export earnings has allowed Russia to increase its foreign exchange reserves from $12 billion in 1999 to about $315 billion in 2006, the third largest reserves in the world and then to $470 billion as on December, 2007. The country is also benefiting from the rising oil prices and has been able to substantially reduce its formerly high foreign debt. The federal budget has shown surpluses since 2001 and in 2006, had a surplus of 9% of GDP.

A simple streamlined tax code adopted in 2001 reduced the tax burden on the people and also increased state revenue. Russia has a flat income tax rate of 13%. It is ranked as the second most attractive tax system in the world after UAE. The implementation has been so successful that it has been emulated by other countries.

Geographically the economic development of the country has been highly uneven. The Moscow region is an affluent region and contributes a disportionately high amount of the GDP. The rest of the country especially the indigenous and rural communities lag behind significantly. Nevertheless, the middle class has increased from just 8 million in 2000 to 55 million in 2006. Russia is well ahead of most other resource-rich countries in its economic development with a long tradition of education, science and industry.

2.3.1 Population

Russia has a population of 141,377,752 (2007 estimate) and faces a negative growth rate of –0.454%. Low birth rate (10.92 births per 1000 population in 2007 estimate) and high death rate (16.04 deaths per 1000 population in 2007 estimate) has reduced Russia's population at 0.5 % annually (750,000 to 800,000 people per year during late 1990's and most of 2000's.) The UN has warned that

Russia's 2005 population could fall by a third by 2050. Government's measures to halt the democratic crisis were a key subject in Putin's nation's address in 2007. A national programme was developed to reverse the trend and a study in 2007 showed that the rate of population decrease has slowed down. The Russian Ministry of Economic Development hopes that by 2020, the population would stabilize at 138-139 million and by 2025 increase again to the present day status.

The country has a high literacy rate of 99.4% for the country as a whole and 99.7% literacy among the males and 99.2% among the females (2002 census.) The UNDP has ranked Russia as the 67th among 177 countries listed.[1]

2.3.2 Health

Russia has more physicians, hospitals and health care workers than almost any other country in the world. However since the collapse of the Soviet Union, the health of the Russian people has declined considerably due to the social, economic and lifestyle changes. According to the 2008 estimates, the average life expectancy in Russia is 59.19 years for males and 73.1 years for females.[2] The main factor contributing to the relatively low life expectancy for males is a high mortality rate among the working age males from preventable causes such as alcohol, smoking, traffic accidents, stress and violent crimes.

Heart diseases account for 56.7% of the total deaths with 30% still in the working age. About 16 million Russians suffer from cardiovascular diseases, making Russia the second in the world in this respect (the first being Ukraine) the mortality rate in Russia is four to five times higher than in Europe.

According to official statistics, there are currently more than 364,000 people in Russia with HIV, but independent sources place the number significantly higher. The World Fact Book places the figure as high as 860,000 people. The government has increased

1 World Fact Book – Russia

2 World Fact book- Russia

spending on HIV control measures by twenty fold in 2006 in order to combat the disease. There has also been an increase of deaths from tuberculosis, particularly among the prison inmates.

In an effort to help improve the demographic situation in Russia, the government has implemented a numbers of programmes designed to increase the birth rate. The monthly child payments have been doubled and since 2007, the government has offered a one time payment of 250,000 Rubles to women who had a second child. In 2007, the country witnessed the highest birth rate ever since the Soviet fall.[3]

2.3.3 Environment

The Soviet and Russian environmental record has been generally dismal. Seven decades of Soviet rule left irradiated landscapes and marine ecosystems, a desiccated inland sea, befouled rivers, and toxic urban air as reminders of the consequences of seeking industrialization at any price. Russia and the other Soviet republics responded to the pressures of the long and costly Cold War by developing a defense-oriented, production-obsessed economy amid ecological devastation. Without a genuine environmental movement until its final years, the Soviet Union left in its wake an environmental catastrophe that will take decades and perhaps trillions of dollars to repair even partially.

2.4 SECTORAL GROWTH

2.4.1 Agriculture

After the fall of the Soviet Union, the large state farms have to deal with the sudden loss of heavy government subsidies. The economic reforms reduced the livestock stock reducing the need for imports of feed grains, soybean and meal. At the same time, imports of meat and other high value products such as processed food, fruits and beverages grew considerably. The 1998 economic

3 Economic Times, "Russian Policies ignite unprecedented birth rate in 2007' 2 February 2008

crisis reduced Russia's ability to import food. After falling to extremely low levels in late 1998, agriculture imports rebounded in 1999.

The use of mineral fertilizer and other costly inputs plummeted, driving yields downward. Most farms could no longer afford to purchase new machinery and other capital investments. After about ten years of decline, Russian agriculture began to show signs of modest improvement. The transition to a more market-oriented system has introduced the element of fiscal responsibility, which has resulted in increased efficiency as farmers try to maintain productivity while struggling with resource constraints. Primary agriculture in Russia continues to be dominated by inefficient, soviet-type collective farms with outdated technology, management skills and strong political connections. One of the main problems Russian farmers are facing is the shortage of agricultural machinery. Russia's machinery is in poor condition and is deteriorating faster than is being replaced. Most of the new machinery is obtained through leasing arrangement funded by the federal government and local administration. The infrastructure is also underdeveloped including transport services, distribution networks and financial services.

Crops: Grains are among Russia's most important crops, occupying more than 50% of cropland. Wheat is dominant in most grain-producing areas. Winter wheat is cultivated in the North Caucasus and spring wheat in the Don Basin, in the middle Volga region, and in southwestern Siberia. Although Khrushchev expanded the cultivation of corn for livestock feed, that crop is only suitable for growth in the North Caucasus, and production levels have remained low compared with other grains. Barley, second to wheat in gross yield, is grown mainly for animal feed and beer production in colder regions as far north as 65° north latitude (the latitude of Arkhangel'sk) and well into the highlands of southern Siberia. Production of oats, which once ranked third among Russia's grains, has declined as machines have replaced horses in farming operations.

Legumes became a common crop in state farms in the 1980s. Potatoes, a vital crop for food and for the production of vodka, are grown in colder regions between 50° and 60° north latitude. Sugar beet production has expanded in recent years; the beets are grown mainly in the rich black-earth districts of European Russia. Flax, also a plant tolerant of cold and poor soils, is Russia's most important raw material for textiles, and the country produced about half the world's flax crop in the 1980s. Flax also yields linseed oil, which together with sunflowers (in the North Caucasus) and soybeans (in the Far East) is an important source of vegetable oil. Production of fruits and vegetables increased as private farms began to expand around 1990. In the mid-1990s, the largest yields in that category were in cabbages, apples, tomatoes, and carrots.

Increased production of fodder crops and expansion of pastureland have supported Russia's livestock industry, although economic conditions have caused cutbacks in animal holdings. Cattle are the most common form of livestock except in the drier areas, where sheep and goats dominate. The third-largest category is pigs, which are raised in areas of European Russia and the Pacific coast that offer grain, potatoes, or sugar beets as fodder. Only very small numbers of chickens are kept, and frozen chicken has become one of Russia's largest import items.

Agricultural reform has proved to be a tough challenge for Russia during its transition to a market economy. The challenge comes from the legacy of the Soviet period and from deeply imbedded cultural biases against individualism. Because of agriculture's vital economic role, large-scale agricultural reform is necessary for success in other sectors. In the mid-1990s, however, private initiative was not rewarded, and inefficient input distribution and marketing structures failed to take advantage of agricultural assets.

Soviet Policy Under Stalin, the government socialized agriculture and created a massive bureaucracy to administer policy. Stalin's campaign of forced collectivization, which began in 1929, confiscated the land, machinery, livestock, and grain stores of the peasantry. By 1937 the government had organized approximately 99 % of the Soviet countryside into state-run collective farms. Under this grossly inefficient system, agricultural yields declined rather than increased. The situation persisted into the 1980s, when Soviet farmers averaged about 10% of the output of their counterparts in the United States. During Stalin's regime, the government assigned virtually all farmland to one of two basic agricultural production organizations—state farms and collective farms. The state farm was conceived in 1918 as the ideal model for socialist agriculture. It was to be a large, modern enterprise directed and financed by the government. The work force of the state farm received wages and social benefits comparable to those enjoyed by industrial workers. By contrast, the collective farm was a self-financed producer cooperative that farmed parcels of land that the state granted to it rent-free and that paid its members according to their contribution of work.

In their early stages, the two types of organization also functioned differently in the distribution of agricultural goods. State farms delivered their entire output to state procurement agencies in response to state production quotas. Collective farms also received quotas, but they were free to sell excess output in collective-farm markets where prices were determined by supply and demand. The distinction between the two types of farms gradually narrowed, and the government converted many collective farms to state farms, where the state had more control.

Private plots also played a role in the Soviet agricultural system. The government allotted small plots to individual farming households to produce food for their own use and for sale as an income supplement. Throughout the Soviet period, the productivity rates of private plots far exceeded their size. With only 3 percent of total sown area in the 1980s, they produced over a quarter of agricultural output.

A number of factors made the Soviet collectivized system inefficient throughout its history. Because farmers were paid the same wages regardless of productivity, there was no incentive to work harder and more efficiently. Administrators who were unaware of the needs and capabilities of the individual farms decided input allocation and output levels, and the high degree of subsidization eliminated incentives to adopt more efficient production methods.

The **Gorbachev agricultural reform program** aimed to improve production incentives. Gorbachev sought to increase agricultural labor productivity by forming contract brigades consisting of ten to thirty farm workers who managed a piece of land leased from a state or collective farm. The brigades were responsible for the yield of the land, which in turn determined their remuneration. After 1987 the government legalized family contract brigades and long-term leasing of land, removing the restrictions on the size of private agricultural plots and cutting into the state's holdings of arable land.

Although Gorbachev's reforms increased output in the agricultural sector in 1986, they failed to address fundamental problems of the system, such as the government's continued control over the prices of agricultural commodities, the distribution of agricultural inputs, and production and investment decisions. In the contract brigade system, farmers still had no real vested interest in the farms on which they worked, and production suffered accordingly. In the 1980s, the Soviet Union went from being self-sufficient in food production to becoming a net food importer.

The **Yeltsin regime** has attempted to address some of the fundamental reform issues of Russian agriculture. But agricultural reform has moved very slowly, causing output to decline steadily through the mid-1990s. Reform began in Russia shortly before the final collapse of the Soviet Union. In December 1990, the Congress of People's Deputies of the Russian Republic enacted a number of laws that were designed to restructure the agricultural sector and make it more commercially viable. The Law on Peasant Farms legalized private farms and allowed them to operate alongside state and collective farms, to hire labor, and to sell produce without state supervision. The same session of the congress passed the Law on Land Reform, which permitted land to be bequeathed as an inheritance from one generation to the next, but not to be bought or sold. The government also established the State Committee for Agrarian Reform, whose responsibility was to oversee the transfer of available land to private farming.

The main thrust of Yeltsin's agricultural reform has been toward reorganizing state and collective farms into more efficient, market-oriented units. A decree of December 1991 and its subsequent amendments provided several options to state and collective farmers for the future structure of their farms. The decree required that farmers choose either to reorganize into joint-stock companies, cooperatives, or individual private farms, or to maintain their existing structure. Under the first two arrangements, workers would hold shares in the farms and be responsible for managing the enterprises. An individual farmer could later decide to break from the larger unit and establish private ownership of his or her share of the land, as determined by an established procedure.

This restructuring program has progressed slowly. Although 95 % of the state and collective farms underwent some form of reorganization, about one-third of them retained essentially their earlier structure. Most of the others, fearing the unstable conditions of market supply and demand that faced individual entrepreneurs, chose a form of collective ownership, either as joint-stock companies or as cooperatives. The conservatism of Russia's farmers prompted them to preserve as much as possible of the inefficient but secure Soviet-era controlled relationships of supply and output.

As of 1996, individual private farming had not assumed the significance in Russian agriculture that reformers and Western supporters had envisioned. Although the number of private farms increased considerably following the reforms of 1990, by the early 1990s the growth of farms had stalled, and by the mid-1990s the number of private farms actually may have dropped as some individuals opted to return to a form of cooperative enterprise or left farming entirely. By the end of 1995, Russia's 280,000 private farms accounted for only 5% of the arable land in Russia.

A number of factors have contributed to the slow progress of agricultural reform. Until the mid-1990s, the state government continued to act as the chief marketing agent for the food sector by establishing fixed orders for goods, thus guaranteeing farmers a market. The government also subsidized farms through guaranteed prices, which reduced the incentive of farmers to become efficient producers.

Perhaps most important, effective land reform has not been accomplished in Russia. The original land reform law and subsequent decrees did not provide a clear definition of private property, and they did not prescribe landholders' rights and protections. The nebulous status of private landholders under the new legislation made farmers reluctant to take the risk of proprietorship. In March 1996, President Yeltsin issued a decree that allows farmers to buy and sell land. However, in April 1996 the State Duma, heavily, influenced by the anti-reform KPRF (Kommunisticheskaya partiya Rossiyskoy Federatsii—KPRF) and its ally, the Agrarian Party of Russia (representing the still formidable vested interests of collective and state farms), passed a draft law that prohibits land sales by anyone but the state. Recent opposition to the new notion of private landownership is based in a strong traditional Russian view that land must be held as collective rather than individual property.

However, in 1996 several factors were exerting pressure on the agricultural sector to become commercially viable. The federal government has retreated from its role as a guaranteed purchaser and marketer, although some regional governments are stepping in to fill the role. And private markets are emerging slowly. Increasingly, Russian agricultural production must compete with imported goods as the gap between domestic prices and world prices narrows. In addition, the fiscal position of the federal government has forced it to reduce subsidies to many sectors of the economy, including agriculture. Subsidies are among the targets of major budget cuts to comply with the standards of the IMF and other Western lenders and achieve macroeconomic stabilization.

One of the most critical problems facing Russian agriculture, and probably the most difficult to solve because of the high cost, is the shortage of agricultural machinery. Russia's fleet of machinery is in **poor condition** and machinery is deteriorating faster than it is being replaced. Most new machinery is obtained through leasing arrangements funded by the federal government and local (oblast) administrations. Since over half of Russia's farms are saddled with considerable debt and few farms are able to offer sufficient collateral to secure large, long-term loans, the purchase of agricultural machinery and **grain-storage facilities** is difficult.

Putin administration has assigned a higher priority to agriculture than Yeltsin had. In July 2000 the Ministry of Agriculture announced a list of basic directions for agriculture, which shifted state priorities away from small private farms and toward large farms and contained a number of measures to stabilize the agricultural sector and increase production. Under Putin agriculture has been recognized as an important sector worthy of state attention and support. In line with the idea of "food security" that has won increasing support since 1995, the revival of food production is considered a strategic policy direction. The Yeltsin-era policy of trying to break up the large formerly collective and state farms into small family farms has been abandoned. The future of Russian agriculture is now seen to lie in large farms vertically integrated with the food-processing industry.

Specific policy initiatives include: The creation of a special division within the agriculture ministry to provide crop insurance for grain, oilseed, sugar beet, and flax against pests, bad weather, and natural disasters, with half of the premiums paid by the government.

- State intervention in the grain market to prevent prices from falling below 2,300 rubles per ton (R2bn were allocated in the 2001 federal budget for this purpose; Gordeyev may seek to increase this to R5-6bn.)
- Greater use of tariffs and quotas to restrict food imports in the interest of the domestic producer. So far sugar producers have acquired the best protection (annual import quota of 3.5m tons and tariffs up to 45 %). A similar quota is being considered for rice. The banning of food imports from both

Europe and the Far East on sanitary grounds also serves protectionist as well as public health purposes.

- Relief of debt accumulated by farms during the 1990s. However, blanket forgiveness of debt (as in the past) is not envisaged; instead, debt is to be restructured on certain conditions.
- Unprofitable farms with good prospects will receive financial support subject to their fulfillment of agreed terms. Unprofitable farms with poor prospects will be disbanded and their land and property distributed among neighboring farms.
- A "new" system of agricultural credit (actually an old system that has been restored) was announced by Gordeyev in 2000 and put into effect in 2001. State credits are transferred to the Russian Agricultural Bank (Rossel'khozbank), the Savings Bank (Sberbank), and other Moscow banks, which then provide loans to farms at subsidized interest rates for the purchase of needed inputs or to fund operations. Professor Wegren questions whether such arrangements can create an effective market infrastructure in the countryside.

2.4.2 Industry

Major manufacturing industries include crude steel, cars and trucks, aircraft, machine equipment, chemicals (including fertilizers), plastics, cement and other building materials, medical and scientific instruments, textiles, handicrafts, paper, television sets, appliances and foodstuffs.

Steel production remains a key industry. Once the world leader in the production of steel, Russian industry fell on hard times in the 1980s as Soviet-made products could not keep up with the quality or output of competitors. Nonetheless, plants continue to operate although less than half use updated equipment. Aluminum and nickel production continue, particularly in mineral rich Siberia. The largest companies are the Noril'sk Nickel Joint-Stock

Company, Bratsk Aluminum, Krasnoyarsk Aluminum, and Sayan Aluminum. European Russia and the Ural region continue to serve as the center for the production of textiles and machine industry. Chemical production is scattered throughout the country, while the center of the oil and gas industry remains the region of the Caucasus Mountains and Caspian Sea. The oil industry was dominated in 2002 by 11 large companies, which accounted for around 90% of production and close to 80% of refining. Russia had 42 oil refineries in 2002, with a total capacity of 5,436,000 barrels per day.

Industrial expansion is mainly in consumer goods and food processing, often embraced by enterprises converting from military production, which dominated industry output in the former Soviet Union.

Russia's industrial base is outmoded and must be restructured or replaced in order for the country to maintain strong economic growth. Nonetheless, Russia emerged from its 1998 economic crisis with an industrial growth rate of 5.2% in 2001. That year, industry accounted for 39% of GDP and employed 28% of the work force. Oil, fuel, and gas made up 54% of Russia's exports in 2000, followed by iron and steel, aluminum, precious metals and stones, and machinery and equipment. Other industrial areas of growth in the early 2000s include construction, automotive equipment, aircraft, and food processing. Russia produced 1,249,582 automobiles in 2001, a 4% increase over 2000. In 2000, it produced 44,123 heavy trucks, a 22% increase over 1999.

2.4.3 Financial institutions

In 1991, when the first Russian stock market was established, trading activity was low. There were only few private companies that existed to offer their shares. The market received a large boost form the privatization programme of the government. The newly privatized firms issued shares and at the same time, a secondary market for the privatization vouchers also emerged. As the first phase of the privatization programme ended the private firms need for capital also increased and an efficient financial market became essential. However the Russian laws and regulations failed to keep pace with the development in the financial markets. This led to gross irregularities. The case of the MMM investment company where small investors were promised huge returns, brought into limelight the lack of western style laws in the Russian legal system. The securities market also lacks a modern communications infrastructure that leads to delays in registration and reporting financial transaction. In 1993, the government began to issue treasury bonds to help finance budget deficits. At selected banks, the people could buy and sell rubles for foreign currency. The Moscow International Currency Exchange (MICEX) establishes the exchange rate through weekly auctions.

According to experts, Russia's new financial institutions are likely to face an adjustment period where weaker banks would either close or merge with strong banks. A regulatory framework must be developed so that people may have confidence in the banking system.

2.4.4 Foreign Investment

In the first half of 2007, foreign investment in Russia doubled year on year reaching $60.3 billion. In 2000, total investment in fixed assets was $40 billion, giving growth of 300% by 2006 when it reached $120 billion. Although the opportunities for investment in Russia are immense yet the FDI's remain far short of the needs of the economy. The cumulative figure from 1991 to 2001 is around $ 18.2 billion or only 5% of domestic fixed capital formation. Russia is most actively encouraging the participation of foreign companies in the oil and gas sector, not only for their capital formation but also for their advanced technology. One possible, though cynical explanation for low levels of FDI is that Russia does not trust the outside world. It would take time to overcome the years of isolation that the country was used to in the days of the Union. Another explanation given is that the banking sector does not have the resources, the capabilities or the trust of the people needed to attract savings that can be directed to productive investments.1

1 www.infoplease.com/country/ profiles/Russia/html

Economists are of the view that Russian economy of today is much smaller than that existed earlier under communism mainly due to the widespread corruption within the government and industry. Those who had the resources and wealth during communism are unwilling to give them up. Financial institutions were not stable enough to handle the sudden privatizations and few had capital to provide the consumers with the amounts they wanted. The shaky confidence caused much FDI to withdraw.

2.4.5 Privatization

The main essence of Russia's economic restructure programme is the Privatization that began in October 1991. In 1992, small enterprises were privatized through employee buyouts and public auctions. By the end of 1993, more than 85% or 82,000 small enterprises were privatized.

In 1992, vouchers were distributed each worth 10,000 ruble to 144 million Russians in order to buy shares in the medium and large-scale enterprises. These vouchers could also be sold, values depending on the economic and political conditions of the economy. By the end of 1994, voucher privatization programme had completed its first phase. About 70% of Russia's medium enterprises were now in private hands.

The next phase of the programme consisted of directly selling the shares for cash in the remaining state enterprises. This was met with stiff opposition from the state Duma and President Yeltsin implemented it by decree. However this only led to worsening of the political conditions. Corruption charges and scandals tarnished the image of the Programme. By 1995, it had gained a negative reputation and the people gave it a slang word prikhvatizatsiya - a combination of the Russian word for "grab" and the Russianized English word "privatize," producing the equivalent of "grabification." The term reflects the belief that privatization has led to the control of the enterprises in the hands of a few individuals with political connections, the mafia or both.

Inspite of all the troubles the second phase went on and was almost completed by 1996. However the government failed to generate the expected revenue. In February 1996, a full-scale investigation into the Privatization Programme was launched by the Procuracy and the government admitted that the programme was handled badly. After Yeltsin's reelection, the Programme was continued with new focus on ten-fifteen large state enterprises.

Despite periodic delays, poor administration and allegations of corruption international experts have judged the programme to be a success. The movement of capital from the hands of the State to private hands has progressed without any serious reversal of direction. This has contributed to a new class of private entrepreneurs.

2.4.6 Russia and the World Trade Organisation

Russia applied for membership in the General Agreement on Tariffs and Trade (GATT) in 1993, but throughout the 1990s negotiations were slow and formal. From 2000 to 2003 President Vladimir Putin made Russia's World Trade Organization (WTO) accession one of his key priorities, but after he failed to reach his self-imposed deadline of 2003, his interest wavered. Russia is already a market economy so WTO membership does not imply systemic changes as great as in China. Given that Russia's primary export products are not sensitive to protectionist measures, WTO membership is also of less economic significance, but the positive effects on the Russian economy from WTO accession would be substantial.

One explanation for Russia's new interest in the WTO was intellectual maturity. Several of the internationally oriented Russian economists and economic politicians had realized the significance of the WTO for Russia, and finally they managed to make it state policy. Possibly, China's entering the WTO was the decisive reason for Russia's turnaround. Russians started wondering if they had missed out on something important when China and the West paid so much attention to China's accession to the WTO. However until the old Ministry of External Economic Relations was abolished nothing much could be done. It was merged with a number of other ministries into the new giant Ministry of Economic Development and Trade, headed by German Gref. A substantial group of young and competent trade negotiators was developed, which could pursue the WTO negotiations more seriously. Russia's chief trade negotiator is Maxim Medvedkov.

Resistance against Russia's entry to the WTO soon arose. It had four centers. The main opponent of an early WTO entry was the top businessman Oleg Deripaska, CEO of the giant Russian Aluminum company, owner of one of Russia's big car companies, Rospromavto, and previously of one of Russia's big airplane-producing companies. Deripaska's two concerns were protection for the car industry and aviation. He mobilized Russia's car industry in opposition to the WTO, persuading the Russian government to slap prohibitive customs tariffs on second-hand Western cars, the actual competition to obsolete Russian cars. He was also pushing for substantial tariffs on imported civilian airplanes. Deripaska made the standard infant industry argument that these manufacturing industries need a substantial period of transition to adjust to freer trade and that the conditions of entry are more important than an early entry.

Another center of resistance was the Russian Chamber of Commerce and Industry, which represents the old red directors and is chaired by former Prime Minister Yevgeny Primakov. As Deripaska, they argued that Russia primarily exports commodities, which enjoy easy access to the world market in any case. Market access for manufactured goods is not very important, because manufacturers can barely keep up with quickly rising domestic demand, while the opening of the Russian market for more imports of manufactured goods would harm domestic manufacturers. A third industrial lobby that objects to the WTO is agriculture. Minister of Agriculture Alexei Gordeev is a strong and able representative of this protectionist lobby. There are primarily two issues. One is that the WTO accession implies a capping of state aid to agriculture. Although Russian agriculture receives very small subsidies today, the agrarians want to keep the option open for larger subsidies in the future. This issue is determined in the multilateral memorandum, and it will probably be the last issue to be resolved. Animal husbandry raises increasing problems, as one part after the other of this previously devastated sector revives. The Russian veterinary services have raised doubts about Western imports of chicken, pork, and beef. When the European Union slapped quotas on Russia's exports of grain to the European Union in early 2003, Russia responded with the introduction of quotas on various kinds of meats, notably on pork, whose production is also developing swiftly. A fourth restive industrial lobby has been services. It falls into many small parts—intellectual property rights, retail trade, telecommunications, insurance, and banking. The infant industry argument is also used here. The United States has made intellectual property rights a key issue, as Russia is a haven of electronic piracy.

Several studies have examined the effects of WTO entry on the Russian economy. The vast majority of Russian households are expected to gain from WTO accession. According to World Bank assessments, welfare gains to Russia will be equal to 3.3% of Russian GDP in the medium term. In the long run, gains could be as high as 11% of GDP when benefits from an improved investment climate are realized.

The main work that remains is negotiation on the multilateral memorandum for Russia's accession. The most serious conflict in Russia's negotiations with the European Union was Russia's domestic price of natural gas, which has all along been much lower than the Russian export prices, which vary greatly with country of destination. This however was settled on conditions favorable to Russia when the European Union signed its bilateral protocol with Russia, a milestone that was reached in May 2004. The remaining obstacle is the Russian embargos against the two WTO members Georgia and Moldova, prohibiting substantial imports of wine and fruits from these two countries, citing sanitary problems. The real issue between these two countries and Russia is the status of the separatist territories, Transnistria in Moldova and Abkhazia and South Ossetia in Georgia. Russian-friendly leaders rule these territories, and Putin has repeatedly suggested that they should become independent. If Russia does not cease its embargos against Georgia and Moldova, these countries have little choice but to refuse to conclude bilateral protocols with Russia. These two countries could either mobilize other WTO members against Russia's accession or stop at precluding their relations with Russia to be covered by the WTO. Finally, the question is whether rising Russian threats to withdraw its WTO application are serious or not. On the one hand, Putin has been the stalwart behind Russia's approach to the WTO, and he recently overruled the agrarian lobby in the bilateral negotiations with the United States on the WTO. On the other hand, as Russian politics have become authoritarian and the oil prices have risen, Russia's commitment to integration with the world economy has weakened.

2.5 EMERGING TECHNOLOGIES IN RUSSIA

2.5.1 Genetic Engineering

Human Genome Project in Russia began in 1988 when a group of researchers led by Bayev asked Gorbachov for support and the scientific community were organized and stared functioning. In Russia, presently there are three approaches in the gene therapy section- gene pathology, gene diagnostics and gene therapy proper. The gene therapy program in Russia is at the initial stage of development. Several genetic centers are engaged in the diagnostics of 23 hereditary diseases. At present the focus is on improving human health by studying the molecular and cellular aspects of the disease and establishing technology for carrying out somatic gene therapy treatment. No legislative norms have been framed for genetic screening and gene therapy so far. The Committee is engaged in formulating guidelines for protocols for clinical trials.[1]

The Russian government passed a resolution in 2000 concerning the registration of genetically modified organisms for biosafety. This resolution opens up the way for genetic engineering in Russia.

2.5.2 Robotics and Artificial Intelligence

In Russian railways robots are used to replace humans in carrying

1 Gene therapy and Human genome project, Vijay Kaushik and Boris Yudin

out the difficult maintenance work. According to a statement from the Russian railways, Russian prototype robots surpass foreign-produced robots with their technical characteristics. However the low level of intellectual and other property rights protection is holding the country back, according to Global Information Technology.[1] Russia ranked 70th out of the 122 countries studied in its assessment of "the impact of information and communication technology on the development process and the competitiveness of nation for the year 2006-07". The country improved its position by two places due to its high capacity for innovation and more widespread Internet use by business firms.

2.5.3 Information Technology

At a meeting of the Information Technology and Communications Ministry, 2008, the Deputy Prime Minister Sergei Ivanov announced a system of 'electronic government' to be created in Russia over the next two years. The government's priority was to create a state information center and access to the data of government information systems. By 2010, all federal and government agencies will have their own websites, meeting single standards.[2]

On February 16th, 2006 President Putin stressed the importance of ICT in the development of the country while addressing the State Council Presidium Meeting on Information and Communication Technology. All citizens and organization need to have equal access to modern technology and there is a need to bridge the gap in communication infrastructure across the nation.

Russia is investing a significant portion of its educational budget on developing Information and Communication technologies in schools, vocational and higher education schools. This is done to reform the educational system and to help Russia

1 "Weak property rights hold back Russian IT" by Tai Aelaja in Moscow Times, March 2007

2 "Russia to create E government systems, http//top.rbc.ru/English/index.shtml?/news/English/2008/02/11/11143154_bod.shtml

catch up with other countries. The government plans to start a federal project e-Russia that aims to increase the diffusion of modern technology. In Russia the effects of digital divide are being felt at all levels- one that separates urban and rural students and a second one that divides rich from the poor students. Ironically the Soviet Union was the first to introduce computer access in schools with a strong emphasis on programming. At the beginning of the 1990's up to 28% of the schools were equipped with computers. However, the situation is different now. Access is scattered and biased. On an average Russian children feel less comfortable handling computers than children from other countries. The spread of ICT is a difficult task for Russia. The huge land mass, thinly spread population lack of available finances and regional diversity has already created problems of effective connectivity and digital networks.[1]

2.5.4 Nanotechnology

Russia is trying to catch up with the West in the field of nanoscience research and is budgeting billions to this effect. However the business sector does not seem to be much interested in the field. A state nanotechnology corporation Rosnanotekh, with a budget of five billion dollars (3.7 billion euros) has been proposed to be set up that will bring in the long needed funds into the neglected establishment. The Russian economy has since woken up to the potential of nanotechnology. Among the most frequently cited applications of nanotechnology are in the metal sector, medicine and molecular chemistry. As the President rightly said, nanotechnologies are becoming the key direction for the development of modern industry and science. In the early 2007, Russia approved a development programme for nanotechnology aimed at achieving and sustaining equality with leading countries in a series of key technologies and sciences. The programme is to run till 2015.[2]

1 The World Bank, Russia Country Department Economics Unit.

2 'Russia to redirect billions in major nanotechnology push' by Dario Thurburn, June 06, 2007

The Ministry of Science and Technology contributes to nanotechnology (NT) through several of its specific programs:

- "Electronic and Optical Properties of Nanostructures" involving a network of large scientific centers (the Ioffe Institute in St. Petersburg, the Lebedev Institute in Moscow, Moscow State University, the Novgograd Institute of Microstructures, the Novosibirsk Institute of Semiconductor Physics, and others). This research network has an annual meeting "Nanostructures, Physics, and Technology" (last held in 1997). It interacts with the Phantom network in the European Community (EC).
- "Solid State Physics" program.
- "Modern Problems of Surface Science," including the vacuum community. A new journal, the Journal of Physics of Low Dimensional Structures, describes well the work performed in the program.
- "Fullerene and nanotubes," in the Physical Chemistry section.
- "Biology," with relatively low contents in nano-biotechnology.
- "Advanced materials," with only several projects related to nanotechnology.

The Russian government and international organizations are the primary research sponsors for nanotechnology in Russia. However, laboratories and companies privatized in the last few years, such as the Delta Research Institute in Moscow, are playing an increasingly active role. The research focus is on advanced processing and continuum modeling and, to a lesser extent, characterization and advanced computing. Especially noteworthy are the achievements made in physico-chemistry and in innovative processing methods.

In the field of medicine, Russian scientist claim to have made an amazing discovery to cure cancer. The disease is considered to be incurable - detection at early stages being very difficult and later stages only 10% are cured. However the situation is set to change now. A microchip has been devised that can detect a predisposition to cancer. It has over one hundred test micro cells concentrated in one square millimeter. Although the chip is still undergoing stringent test, scientist are confident of its success. The most attractive feature of the chip is its low price. Even poor clinics intend to buy these chips.[1]

2.6 LINKAGES

As a rapidly emerging economy Russia is struggling to curb its galloping inflation rates. The high inflation rates promotes banks to increase interest rates that attracts more speculative capital and also hampers the country's competitiveness by making imports cheaper. Reducing inflation is a priority for Russia to improve long term investment in industry. The rates of inflation dropped from over 20% in 2000 when Putin came to power to 9% in 2006. Inflation stood at 11.9% in 2007. According to Putin, international prices and the rising production of biofuel is responsible for the increase in prices.

According to economists in Forbes, the Russian economy is overheating. Unemployment has been decreasing since 2003 and real wages have accelerated. Reports of strikes and protests for higher pay or other benefits indicate increased worker activism and also indicate the shortage of skilled workers. The overall pool of manpower is shrinking. A wage price spiral has pushed inflation to a very high risk in Russia. As oil prices increased, rapidly improving the terms of trade has pushed aggregate demand to outpace the production growth. The culmination of all this has been the galloping inflation rate.

In order to control the increasing prices of food grains, Russia needs to develop its own stock. Currently only 4.6% of the people are engaged in agriculture and contribute 10.8% of GDP. Russia,

1 Nanotechnology to cure cancer (Russia) by alexandr Saenko on November 20, 2007 in Science: http://en.mykinda.com

although huge in size has vast land uncultivable like Siberia and the Artic region. Therefore the challenge to the Russian Scientists is to maximize the production on the available land. The crisis of 1998 affected agriculture severely. The economic transition to the market system left the farmers unable to afford fertilizers or any new machinery. As a result, Russian agriculture has outdated technology and poor yield. Genetic engineering in agriculture seems to be the solution for Russia. Already a GM variety of Potato 'Elisabeth' has been approved by the Chief Sanitation Doctor of Russian Federation. Potato is a vital crop for Russia both as a food crop as well as for the production of Vodka. Agricultural reform is thus a tough challenge and one that Russia needs to develop as an economic superpower.

The application of robotics and artificial intelligence can help revive Russia's steel production industry. The industry was once the world leader and had fallen on bad times in the 1980's. Applying the technology can help in cutting costs and improving productivity.

3 INDIA

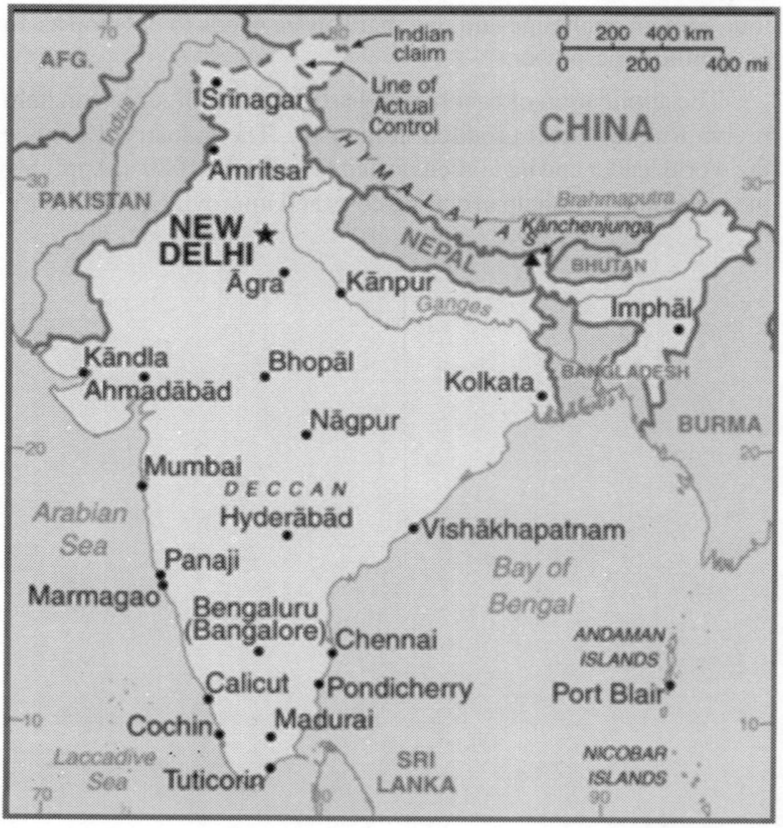
Indian claim
Line of Actual Control
0 200 400 km
0 200 400 mi
AFG.
Srinagar
Amritsar
CHINA
PAKISTAN
NEW DELHI
Āgra
Kānpur
HIMALAYA
NEPAL
Kānchenjunga
BHUTAN
Brahmaputra
Ganges
Imphāl
Indus
Kāndla
Ahmadābād
Bhopāl
Kolkata
BANGLADESH
Nāgpur
BURMA
Mumbai
DECCAN
Arabian Sea
Hyderābād
Vishākhapatnam
Panaji
Marmagao
Bay of Bengal
Bengaluru (Bangalore)
Chennai
ANDAMAN ISLANDS
Calicut
Pondicherry
Port Blair
Cochin
Madurai
Laccadive Sea
Tuticorin
SRI LANKA
NICOBAR ISLANDS

Capital	— New Delhi
Area	— 3,287,590 sq. km
Population	— 1,147,995,904 (July 2008est.)
Average rate of growth of population	— 1.578%
Currency	— Indian Rupee (INR)
GDP(PPP)	— $ 2.966 trillion(2007)
GDP (per capita PPP)	— $ 2,600 (2007)
GDP real growth rate	— 9 % (2007)
Agriculture as a share of GDP	— 17.8% (2007)
Exports	— $151.3 billion (2007)
Life Expectancy at birth	— 69.25 years (2008)
Infant mortality rate	— 32.31 deaths/1000 live birth (2008 est.)
Literacy	— 61% (2004)
Human Development Index	— 0.169 rank 128th

The Republic of India is located in South Asia. It is the seventh largest country in geographical area, the second most populous country and the largest democratic country of the world. India sits atop the Indian tectonic plate. The geological process began seventy five million years ago when the Indian subcontinent, then a part of the southern super continent Gondwana began a northeast ward drift. The subsequent collision with the Eurasian Plate gave rise to the Himalayas, the highest mountains on planet Earth. India's climate is strongly influenced by the Himalayas and the Thar Desert, both of which drives the monsoons. The Himalayas prevent the cold winds from blowing in and the Thar Desert attracts the moisture-laden winds that provide most of India's rainfall.

With a population of 1,129,866,154 (2007 est.), India suffers from substantial poverty. The Planning Commission of India has estimated that 27.5 % of the people were living below the poverty line. The wealth distribution in India is also uneven with the top 10% earning 33 % of the income. More than ¼ of the country earn less than $0.40 per day.

India lies in the Indomalaya ecozone and has significant biodiversity. India's forest cover ranges from the tropical rainforest of the Andaman Islands, Western Ghats and northeast India to the coniferous forests of the Himalayas. The country contains 172 or 2.9 % of IUCn designated threatened species including the Asiatic Lion, the Bengal Tiger and the Indian white-rumped vulture.

3.1 BRIEF HISTORY

The first known permanent settlements appeared over 9,000 years ago and gradually developed into the Indus Valley Civilisation, dating back to 3300 BC in western India. It was followed by the Vedic Civilisation, which laid the foundation of Hinduism and other cultural aspects of early Indian society.

The empire built by the Maurya dynasty under Emperor Ashoka united most of South Asia in the third century BC. From the third century, the Gupta dynasty oversaw the period referred to as an ancient "India's Golden Age." Between the 10th and 12th centuries, invasions from Central Asia resulted in most of north India coming under the rule of the Delhi Sultanate and later the Mughal dynasty. Meanwhile many indigenous kingdoms also flourished in the South such as the Vijayanagara Empire. In the 17th and 18th century the Mughal supremacy declined and the Maratha Empire became powerful.

The search for wealth and power brought Europeans to the Indian shore in 1498 when Vasco da Gama arrived in Calicut (modern day, Kozhikode, Kerala). In 1510, the Portuguese took over Goa, which became the centre for the commercial and political power in India. Other European companies such as East India Company, England and the United East India Company, Netherlands followed them. Indian rulers readily accommodated the newcomers in the hope of pitting them against the Portuguese. In 1619, the Mugal Emperor Jahangir granted them permission to trade in Surat, Gujarat and Hughli, West Bengal.

English company agents became familiar with the Indian customs and languages. The knowledge thus acquired gave the English the competitive edge over other Europeans. The French commercial interest came late but they also established themselves at Pondicherry on the Coromandel Coast.

By 1856, most of India was under the control of the East India Company. The British success was the result of not only their superior tactics and weapons but also their relation with the Indian rulers through the "subsidiary alliance" system. Many rulers bartered away their real responsibility by agreeing to uphold British supremacy while they retained a fictional sovereignty over their land. Later through the "doctrine of lapse" Dalhousie annexed outright many estates.

The 1850's witnessed the introduction of the three "engines of social improvement" –the railroads, the uniform postal service and the telegraph. The increased ease of communication and the opening of highways and waterways accelerated the movement of troops, the transportation of raw materials and goods to and from the interiors, and the exchange of commercial information.

On May 10, 1857, Indian soldiers of the British Indian Army mutinied in Merrut, a cantonment 80 km from Delhi. The uprising, which seriously threatened the British rule in India, has been referred to as India's first War of Independence. Initially the rebels gained the upper hand; the final outcome was victory for the British.

The civil war was major turning point in the history of modern India. In May 1858, the British exiled Emperor Bahadur Shah II, the last Mughal Emperor. At the same time, the East India Company was abolished and India came under the direct control of the British Crown. The decades following the Rebellion were a period of political awareness, and emergence of Indian leadership at national and provisional levels. Inspired by a suggestion by A.O. Hume, seventy-three Indian delegates founded the Indian National Congress. In 1905, Sir George Curzon, the governor-general ordered the partition of Bengal. Widespread agitation ensued in the streets and the Congress advocated boycotting British products under the banner of Swadeshi. The boycott was so successful that the British tried to resolve the situation by announcing a series of reforms in 1909 and appointing few moderates to provisional councils. In 1911 King George V visited India during which he announced the reversal of the partition of Bengal and the transfer of the capital from Calcutta to a newly planned city, which became New Delhi.

World War I saw an unprecedented outpouring of loyalty and goodwill towards the British. India contributed by providing men and resources. But disillusionment set in early. High causality rates, inflation along with high taxation and the disruption of trade increased human suffering in India. This was compounded by the Rowlatt Acts of 1919. The act gave the government with extraordinary powers to quell sedition by silencing the press, detaining political activities without trial and arresting any suspected individuals without a warrant. A nation wide strike was called by M.K. Gandhi to protest the Act. The agitation culminated on 13th April 1919 in Amritsar, Punjab when Brigadier Reginald Dyer ordered the soldiers to fire at an unsuspecting crowd of 10,000 men women and children. The crowd had assembled at Jallianwala Bagh, a walled garden to celebrate a festival. The incident killing hundreds and wounding thousands dispelled wartime hopes and goodwill.

In 1920, the Congress was reorganized and was given a new goal –Swaraj. In his first nationwide Satyagraha, Gandhi urged the people to boycott British institutions, products, resign from government jobs, and refuse to pay taxes etc. The party became an organization of mass national appeal. In 1930, Gandhi undertook the famous march of 4000 kilometers to Dandi in protest against extortionate British taxes on salt. Their defiance showed India's determination to be free from British rule.

In February 1937, when elections were held, provisional autonomy became a reality. However electoral gains were short lived as the ministers resigned when the Viceroy declared India entry to the World War II without consulting the Indian leaders. Meanwhile the demand for dividing the country into two separate states, one Muslim, the other Hindu was gaining strength.

In the election campaign of 1946 the Congress wasted precious time denouncing the British rather than allaying Muslin fears. When it became clear that Congress did not wish to share power with the

Muslim League, Jinnah declared August 1, 1946 as Direct Action Day. This brought communal rioting and massacre in many parts in the north of the country. Partition seemed preferable to civil war.

On June 3 1947, Viscount Louis Mountbatten announced the partition of British Indian Empire into India and Pakistan. On August 15 1947, India became independent and three years later on 26 January 1950, India became a republic and the new constitution came into effect.

Since independence, India has experienced violence in many parts of the country. The country has unresolved territorial issues with China (in 1962 it turned into the Sino-Indian war) and Pakistan (leading to wars in 1947, 1965, 1971 and 1999)

In 1974, India conducted nuclear tests followed by five more tests in 1998, making India a nuclear state. Since 1991, India has undertaken significant economic reforms making it one of the fastest growing economies of the world.

3.2 GOVERNMENT AND POLITICS

The Constitution of India is the longest and most exhaustive constitution of any independent nation in the world. It came into force on January 26, 1950 and defines India as a sovereign, socialist, secular, democratic republic (the terms socialist and secular was added during the Emergency period). The country has three branches of governance-Legislative, Executive and Judiciary. The President is the head of state elected indirectly by the Electrol College for a five-year term. The Prime Minister is the de facto head of the government and exercises most of the executive powers.

India has a bicarmel parliament operating under a Westminster style parliament. The upper house called Rajya Sabha (Council of States) is a permanent body with up to 250 members serving staggered six-year terms. The lower house called Lok Sabha has 545 members directly elected by popular vote to serve five-year terms.

The Executive branch consists of the President, Vice President and the Council of Ministers, headed by the Prime Minister. In India, the executive is subordinate to the legislature with the Prime Minister and the Council of Ministers directly responsible to the lower house of the Parliament.

The Judiciary has three tiers consisting of the Supreme Court, twenty-one High Courts and a large number of trial courts. The Supreme Court has original jurisdiction over cases involving fundamental rights and over disputes between the Center and the State. The role as the ultimate interpreter of the Constitution is one of the most important functions of the Supreme Court.

Politics For most of its democratic history, India has been led by the Indian National Congress (INC). Other national parties include the Bharatiya Janta Party (BJP), the Communist Party of India (CPI) and various regional parties. From 1950 to 1990, except two brief periods, the INC enjoyed parliamentary majority. Between 1977 and 1980, the Janta Party was in power due to discontent of the people, during the Emergency declared by the then Prime Minister Indira Gandhi. In 1989, a coalition government ruled for two years. Between the years 1996-1998, several short-lived alliances were in sway. In 1998, the BJP formed an alliance with several regional parties to become the first non-Congress government to complete a full five-year term. In 2004 elections the Congress won the largest number of seats in the Lok Sabha and formed the present coalition government led by the Prime Minister Manmohan Singh. The country also has the first woman President Pratibha Patil in the history of the country.

3.3 ECONOMY

India is the world's 12th largest economy—and the third largest in Asia behind Japan and China—with total GDP of around $1 trillion ($1,000 billion). Services, industry, and agriculture account for 55%, 27%, and 18% of GDP respectively. Nearly two-thirds of the population depends on agriculture for its livelihood. Nearly 700 million Indians live on $2 per day or less, but there is a large and growing middle class of 325-350 million with disposable income for consumer goods. India has an HDI ranking of 128th placing the country in a medium category for human development.

India began its process of economic liberalisation in 1991. Before the reform process, India had strict controls on foreign exchange. The idea was to promote and stimulate the domestic production. Reforms included opening up the economy for liberal foreign investments, industrial decontrol, reduction in tariffs and other trade barriers, reforms in the financial sector and so on. The government also made due adjustments in the monetary and fiscal policies.

Real GDP growth for the fiscal year ending March 31, 2007 was 9.4%, up from 9.0% growth in the previous year. Growth for the year ending March 31, 2008 is expected to be between 8.5-9.0%. Foreign portfolio and direct investment inflows have risen significantly in recent years. They have contributed to $255 billion in foreign exchange reserves by June 2007. Government receipts from privatization were about $3 billion in fiscal year 2003-2004, but the privatization program has stalled since then.

Economic growth in India is hampered by inadequate infrastructure, a cumbersome bureaucracy, corruption, labor market rigidities, regulatory and foreign investment controls, the "reservation" of key products for small-scale industries, and high (although declining) fiscal deficits. The outlook for further trade liberalization is mixed. India eliminated quotas on 1,420 consumer imports in 2002 and has incrementally lowered non-agricultural customs duties in recent successive budgets.

The United States is India's largest trading partner. Bilateral trade in 2006 was $32 billion. Principal U.S. exports are diagnostic or lab reagents, aircraft and parts, advanced machinery, cotton, fertilizers, ferrous waste/scrap metal, and computer hardware. Major U.S. imports from India include textiles and ready-made garments, Internet-enabled services, agricultural and related products, gems and jewelry, leather products, and chemicals.

The rapidly growing software sector is boosting service exports and modernizing India's economy. Software exports crossed $28 billion in FY 2006-2007, while business process outsourcing (BPO) revenues hit $8.3 billion in 2006-2007. Personal computer penetration is 14 per 1,000 persons. The cellular/mobile market surged to 140 million subscribers by November 2006. The country has 54 million cable TV customers.

3.3.1 Population

India is the 2nd most densely populated country in the world with 368 persons per square kilometer. Although population continues to be the biggest problem of the country, the median age is 25.1 years making India the youngest country in the world. The burgeoning population continues to increase and exert tremendous pressure on the environment and the fast depleting natural resources. Population projections have indicated that India could overtake China as the world's most populous nation as early as in 2030. However looking at the decreasing population growth rate, demographers believe that the country's population will stabilize well before 2050. In the last 15 yrs, the growth rate of population has decreased from 2.15% to 1.6% indicating that the country is making some progress to stabilize. Moreover, the current fertility rate is 2.8 children per woman, which is not much higher than the replacement level of 2.1 required to stabilize the population.

3.4 SECTORAL GROWTH

3.4.1 Agriculture

Although 48% of the land is arable, and 60% of the population is engaged in the sector, agriculture only contributes16.6% of GDP. (World Fact Book-2007 est.) This huge disproportionality signifies the problem Indian agriculture faces –low productivity. Realizing the importance of this, the Central government has played an active role in improving the sector although constitutionally it is a state responsibility. Planning is centralized; policies and resource allocation are decided at the Central level.

Dependence on agricultural imports during the early 1960's convinced the planners that food self-sufficiency was very crucial for national independence, security and political stability.

There are large disparities among India's states and territories in agricultural performance, only some of which can be attributed to differences in climate or initial endowments of infrastructure such as irrigation. Realizing the importance of agricultural production for economic development, the central government has played an active role in all aspects of agricultural development. Planning is centralized, and plan priorities, policies, and resource allocations are decided at the central level. Food and price policy also are decided by the central government. Thus, although agriculture is constitutionally the responsibility of the states rather than the central government, the latter plays a key role in formulating policy and providing financial resources for agriculture.

Agriculture has always been India's most important economic sector. It provides approximately one-third of the gross domestic product and employs roughly two-thirds of the population. Since independence in 1947, the share of agriculture in the GDP has declined in comparison to the growth of the industrial and services sectors. However, agriculture still provides the bulk of wage goods required by the nonagricultural sector as well as numerous raw materials for industry. Moreover, the direct share of agricultural and allied sectors in total exports is around 18 %. When the indirect share of agricultural products in total exports, such as cotton textiles and jute goods, is taken into account, the percentage is much higher.

Dependence on agricultural imports in the early 1960s convinced planners that India's growing population, as well as concerns about national independence, security, and political stability, required self-sufficiency in food production. This perception led to a program of agricultural improvement called the Green Revolution, to a public distribution system, and to price supports for farmers. In the 1980s, despite three years of meager rainfall and a drought in the middle of the decade, India managed to get along with very few food imports because of the growth in food-grain production and the development of a large buffer stock against potential agricultural shortfalls. By the early 1990s, India was self-sufficient in food-grain production. Agricultural production has kept pace with the food needs of the growing population as the result of increased yields in almost all crops, but especially in cereals. Food grains and pulses account for two-thirds of agricultural production in the mid-1990s. The growth in food-grain production is a result of concentrated efforts to increase all the Green Revolution inputs needed for higher yields: better seed, more fertilizer, improved irrigation, and education of farmers. Although increased irrigation has helped to lessen year-to-year fluctuations in farm production resulting from the vagaries of the monsoons, it has not eliminated those fluctuations.

3.4.2 Industry

Modern industry has advanced fairly rapidly since independence, and the industrial sector now contributes 26.9% of the GDP. Large modern steel mills and many fertilizer plants, heavy machinery plants, oil refineries, locomotive and automotive works have been constructed; the metallurgical, chemical, cement, and oil-refining industries have also expanded. India has also established its role in the high value-added sectors of the "new economy" sectors of information technology (IT), computer hardware, computer software, media and entertainment. However, although the total product is large, industry absorbs only about 17% of the labor force. Nine states— Maharashtra, West Bengal, Tamil Nadu, Gujarat, Uttar Pradesh, Bihar, Andhra Pradesh, Karnataka, and Madhya Pradesh— together account for most of Indian industry.

Industrial production expanded at an average annual rate of 5– 6% between 1970 and 1990. Enforced austerity and demand management measures taken to stabilize rapidly worsening macroeconomic imbalances in 1991–92 slowed growth in the industry sector to 0% for that year. This was followed by a modest recovery to 1.9% growth in 1992–93, though declining to an estimated 1.6% in 1993–94, due to lingering effects of the earlier stabilization measures as well as poorer than expected demand in key export markets. In 1995–96, however, the index of industrial production (IIP) jumped 11.7%, led by a 13% increase in manufacturing output, the highest in 25 years. Growth in industrial production was 6.6% in 1997/98, but slowed to 4.1% in 1998/99 primarily due to the effects of the Asian financial crisis, but also in part to international sanctions imposed after its nuclear tests in 1998. A rebound evidenced in 6.6% growth in 1999/00 was cut short by the global slowdown in 2001, and the aftermath of the 11 September 2001 terrorist attacks on the United States, including intensifying regional tensions with Pakistan. Growth in industrial production slowed, to 5.1% in 2000/01 and to 2.7% in 2001/02.

Under the planned development regime of past decades, government directives channeled much of the country's resources into public enterprises. Private investment was closely regulated for all industries, discouraging investors from formal entry into the sector. However, industrial policy in recent years has shifted towards privatization and deregulation. Since 1991 government licensing requirements have been abolished for all but a few "controlled areas": distillation and brewing of alcoholic drinks, cigars and cigarettes, defense equipment, industrial explosives, hazardous chemicals, and drugs and pharmaceuticals. Under the government disinvestment program announced at the end of 1999, only three sectors remain completely closed to private investment: defense, atomic energy, and railway transport. The oil industry was opened to joint foreign investment in 1997 under the New Exploration and Licensing Policy (NELP). The first exploration blocks were auctioned off in two rounds in 2000, but the initiative none of the major international oil companies put in bids. The Ministry of Disinvestments was established in December 1999 to oversee the reduction of government shares in 247 state-owned companies, referred to as public sector units (PSUs), to a 26% stake. The first sale, in early 2000, was 51% of the Bharat Aluminum Company, Ltd. to Sterlite Ltd. of India. In May 2002, managerial control of Maruti Udyog Ltd. (MUL), India's top carmaker claiming a 60% market share, was transferred to Suzuki Maintenance Corporation (SMC) of Japan, one of the few foreign buyers in the disinvestments program to date. Generally, the PSUs for which the government has found buyers in its disinvestments program have not been in the industrial or manufacturing sectors.

Instead, the government has also steps to make their operations more competitive. In 2001 for instance, quantitative restrictions (QRs) were removed from about 715 imports, including cars, clothes, watches, pins, and dairy products as part of the accession process to the WTO. Credit and capital markets have also been greatly liberalized. Since 1992, all foreign companies have been on par with Indian companies in the area of foreign exchange solvency and on the stock market. With these reforms, private investment in industry is now proceeding at a steady if still modest pace, fostering increased competition in most of the mining and manufacturing sectors previously monopolized by parastatals. In 2001/02 net foreign direct investment (FDI) and net portfolio investment combined equaled $6.3 billion, the highest on record.

Textile production dominates the industrial field, accounting for about 30% of export earnings while adding only 7% to 8% to imports. The textile industry employs approximately 35 million workers, making it the second-largest employer in India after agriculture. The sector is highly fragmented, containing about 7000 operational units encompassing a $2.9 billion clothing industry, a $16.3 billion finished fabrics industry, a $1.9 billion industrial textile products industry, and a $600 million household textile products industry. On a broad level it can also be divided between the natural fiber segment (cotton, silk, wool, jute, etc.) and the man-made fiber segment (polyester filament yarn, blended yarns, etc.). Cotton accounts for about 60% of both domestic consumption and exports. In terms of operations, since the 1980s decentralized power looms have produced an increasingly large share of production as centralized mills have declined. In 1986, there were about 638,000 decentralized power looms in operation, and by 2002 these had increased 260% to about 1,662,000, including an estimated 1,227,000 conventional shuttle looms, 400,000 drop-box semi-automatic looms, 30,000 automatic looms and 5,000 shuttleless looms (most second-hand imports). Anticipating the globalization of the textile market in 2004 when the multifiber agreement (MFA) is scheduled to be phased out, India's National Textile Policy-2000 has pinpointed the weaving sector as the crucial link in the textile value chain (from fiber to fabric to garment to style) that needs to become more competitive. The Textile Program, announced in the budget for 2001/02, included a program for modernizing the powerloom sector through the introduction of 50,000 shuttleless looms and 250,000 semiautomatic looms. The union budget for 2002/03 continued the program, adding an array of tax and duty exemptions for the benefit of powerloom operators. In 2002/03, the Office of the Textile Commissioner estimated that decentralized powerlooms accounted for 76.8% of cloth production (including hosiery); hand looms, 18%; mills, 3.7%; and others, 1.5%. By contrast, integrated mill operations, which perform spinning, weaving and processing in a central location, have stagnated and declined. In December 2002, 464 mills were closed compared to 220 in 1999/98, and hundreds more were slated for closure in 2003. There were 1,782 cotton and man-made fiber mills in 1999; only 192 of them were publicly owned. Mumbai (formerly Bombay), Ahmadabad, and the provincial cities in southern India lead in cotton milling, which accounts for about 65% of the raw material consumed by the textile industry. Jute milling is localized at Calcutta, center of the jute agricultural area. India is the world's largest jute manufacturer. On average, textile production has been growing about 5% a year, although in 2001–02, with demand damped by a series of negative events—economic recession in the United States, a global economic slowdown, the 11 September 2001 terrorist attacks on the United States, the attack on India's Parliament 13 December 2001 and sectarian violence in Gujarat—growth fell to 2.6%, compared with 4.4% in 2000/01, while textile exports fell 9%. However, by the end of 2002 and continuing into 2003 strong growth was evidenced. The production of textile products, including ready-made garments, grew 17% during the first quarter of 2003 year-on-year (YOY) and textile exports grew 8.48%.

India is the world's tenth-largest steel producer. In 2001/02, according to the Ministry of Steel, it produced 4.08 million tons of pig iron (up 19.8%) and 30.64 million tons of finished steel (up 4.7%). The industry consists of seven large integrated mills and about 180 mini steel plants. Despite some signs of recovery 2002, all the major steel companies except the Tata Steel Corporation, the largest and oldest (founded in 1907), were facing serious financial problems due to overcapacity, cheap imports, and anti-dumping duties imposed by the United States in June 2001 that affected Indian exports. Nevertheless, during 2002 steel experienced a strong revival due to rising steel prices, increased domestic demand mainly from highway construction projects, and a 15.88% YOY rise in exports April to November 2002. The metallurgical sector also produced 818,000 tons of aluminum products, up from 640,000 tons in 1998/99. Automobile production, fed by both the steel and aluminum industries, has grown at annual rates of close to 20% since liberalization in 1993, propelled by low interest rates, the expansion of consumer finance, and strong export demand. In 2002, 90.2% of vehicles produced were economy cars, and 9.8% were luxury cars and SUVs. From 1999/2000 to 2001/02, total production of cars, utility vehicles and commercial vehicles declined 4.7% from 875,179 to 834,071, while the production of two-wheelers increased 14.4%, from about 4.8 million to 5.47 million. Exports of all kinds of vehicles totaled 215,318 April to December 2002, a 68% YOY increase.

In the field of computers and consumer electronics production has been boosted by the liberalization of technology and component imports. In consumer durables, production in many cases grew at double-digit rates in 2002/02 (air conditioners, 25%; microwave ovens, over 20%; color TVs, over 15%, refrigerators, 12%; audio products and DVDs, 10%; washing machines, less than 5%), while computer production was up 36%. Computer software exports have grown as a compound growth rate of 50% per year for the past five years. In 2001/02, electronics hardware exports reached $1.253 billion, up 22.6% over 2001/02, while computer software exports reached $7.8 billion, up 28.7%.

In the petrochemical sector, India has 18 refineries throughout the country with a total refinery capacity of more that two million barrels per day. Sixteen refineries are government-owned, one is jointly owned, and one, the 540,000-barrels-per-day Reliance

Industries refinery at Jamnagar in Gujarat State, is privately owned. Almost half India's refinery capacity—now at 970,000 barrels per day—has been built since 1998, the government's goal being self-sufficiency in refined petroleum products. India's total refinery capacity should currently be enough to meet domestic demand, but because of operational problems it still has to import diesel fuel.

India's cement industry is the second largest in the world, after China, with an installed capacity of 135 million tons as of March 2002. Exports have been very limited and only to immediate neighbors. The cement industry is highly fragmented, consisting of 120 large plants and 56 companies. In the last decade, government's portion of cement consumption decreased from 50% to 35% as the domestic housing market has grown. However, government financed infrastructure projects also helped sparked a growth in construction of about 9.7% YOY April to December 2002. In 2001/02, 106.9 million tons of cement was produced, of which 5.14 million tons were exported.

Like cement, India's food processing industry in oriented mainly toward the domestic market. It is India's fifth largest industry, with output reaching $31 billion food in 2001/02. Structurally it consists of about 9000 operational units, accounts for about 6.3% of GDP, 13% of exports, and 18% of industrial employment (about 1.6 million workers).

India's fertilizer industry is the third largest in the world, and central to its efforts to increase agricultural productivity. The industry consists of 64 large fertilizer plants (39 producing urea, the most affordable fertilizer and 18 manufacturing diammonium phosphate or DAP, and other products), and 79 small and medium plants. As of 2000, installed capacity in nitrogen-based nutrients was 11 million tons and in phosphate-based nutrients, 3.6 million tons. Potassium-based nutrients must all be imported. Since 1992 the government has been gradually decontrolling the price of fertilizers. The prices of urea are scheduled to be completely decontrolled by 2006/07.

Overall industrial production grew at 2.7% in 2001/02, its weakest performance since the early 1990s. Manufacturing, accounting for about 80% of the sector, grew 2.9%, while the electricity segment increased 3.1% and mining only 1.2%. Figures for April to November 2002 showed signs of recovery, however, with a 5.3% YOY increase for industrial production overall, and 5.4% YOY growth in manufacturing.

3.4.3 Financial Institutions

India has strong and well-formed financial institutions in the country with a central bank, commercial banks, credit rating agencies, securities board, insurance companies as well as specialized institutions. The central bank better known as the Reserve Bank of India was established in 1935 to felicitate fiscal stability to the economy. It is the regulatory authority and formulates the different rates that improve the banking sector. The bank issues currency notes and offers aid to the central government and its various institutions. The country has a vast range of commercial banks that can be categorized into foreign banks, private banks and public sector banks. There are also specialized banks that provide assistance to different sectors such as the Board for industrial and financial reconstruction, Export-Import Bank of India, and the Small Industries Development Bank of India.

3.4.4 Foreign Direct Investment

In India, Foreign Direct Investment was marginal in the decades leading to economic liberalization. For example, in 1960, FDI was only Rs. 0.5 billion. Only when large-scale reforms took place in 1991 did FDI's take off with US $ 167 million. In 1994-95 it increased to $1,374 million and in 2005-March 2006 it had increased to $5,549 million. The main sectors attracting foreign investments during 2000-2007 are the services sector with $8,974 million (19.84%); the computer sector including both software and hardware with investment of $7,004 million (15.65%); and third the telecommunication sector with foreign investment of $3,623 million (7.99%). The total FDI inflow to India from 1991 to 2007 amounts to $54,628 million. The main participating country in India's FDI inflow is Mauritius. Between 1991 and 2005, the inflows from the country amounted to $11,115.47 million (37.25%) followed by US- $4,912 (15.8%) and Japan-$2,059 (6.79%)

The FDI outflow from India is expected to cross $15 billion – surpassing the inflows to the country. The preferred destinations of investment are found to be the European countries and the US. Africa is also a popular destination. The main sectors attracting the FDI's are- metal, pharmaceuticals, industrial goods, beverages, cosmetics and software & financial services.

India is emerging as a major world player in Cross border Mergers and Acquisitions as an important mode of overseas market entry. During 2000-2003, Indian companies were involved in 182 overseas M&A as compared to just 60 in 1996-99. Indian companies taking over large international enterprises have made headlines across the globe. The UNCTAD report calls this as 'a giant awakening' All this has been possible due to some changes in the RBI guidelines. Earlier the Indian companies could make overseas investment of only 50% of their net worth, subject to a ceiling of $100 million. Since January 2004, Indian companies are allowed to make any amount of overseas investment by market purchases of foreign exchange without prior approval of RBI up to 100% of their net worth without any ceiling whatsoever. Further more, Indian companies can now invest or make acquisitions aboard in areas unrelated to their business at home. The Tata-Corus deal, Arcelor-Mittal deal and more recently the Tata- Jaguar deal are some of the major ones. Equally interesting is the new type of reverse integration of the small company taking over a bigger company.

In UNCTAD outward FDI performance index ranking covering 132 economies, India has improved its ranking from 80 in 1990 to 54th rank in 2004.

3.4.5 ForeignTrade

Initially, India's foreign trade followed a pattern common to all underdeveloped countries: exporting raw materials and food in exchange for manufactured goods. The only difference in India's case was that it also exported processed textiles, yarn, and jute goods. Until the late 1980s, the government's strongly import substitution-oriented industrial policy limited the significance of exports for the Indian economy, and while exports have become more important, they remain only about 8% of national income. With imports exceeding exports almost continuously in the 1970s and 1980s, India registers a chronic trade deficit. Stabilization and structural adjustment measures taken in 1991, including 50% currency devaluation, have improved the country's balance of trade position by depressing imports and making exports more competitive in the world market. Given the country's relatively well-developed manufacturing base, items like textile goods, gems and jewelry, engineering goods, chemicals, and leather manufactures now comprise the country's leading exported items, replacing jute, tea, and other food products that dominated its export base in the 1960s and early 1970s.

In 1999 India's imports were distributed among the following categories: India's exports are dominated by textiles, followed by agricultural products, gems and jewelry, and engineering goods. Major imports include petroleum and petroleum products, gold and precious stones, machinery, chemicals, and fertilizers.

Consumer goods	2.6%
Food	6.8%
Fuels	30.8%
Industrial supplies	40.3%
Machinery	14.2%
Transportation	2.8%
Other	2.4%

3.5 EMERGING TECHNOLOGIES IN INDIA

3.5.1 Genetic Engineering

Genetic technology in plant transformation is affecting crop improvement in unprecedented ways. The new technology promises greater efficiency to plant breeding but also requires careful planning as they have the additional biosafety consideration.

In order to make a good impact, the crops must be chosen carefully and those of national importance. Thus crops that contribute the most to our food and nutritional security (e.g. rice, wheat, chickpea, pigeonpea, groundnut, mustard, tomato, peas, cauliflower, banana, etc.) should be accorded high priority. Similarly, commercial crops such as sugarcane and cotton that provide rural employment and occupy large area also deserve high priority. According to S.R.Bhat and V.L.Chopra another aspect to be kept in mind are the international trade opportunities. Some countries in Europe and Japan are strongly opposing transgenic crops. The case of rice is a good example. Basmati rice enjoys a good international market and is a major foreign exchange earner for India. Therefore it would be wise to hold cultivation of transgenic Basmati and to keep basmati belt area free from transgenetic rice. This measure will be necessary to avoid inadvertent mixture of transgenic and non-transgenic seeds during cultivation, transport or trade. Biosafety concerns are the major reasons for non-adoption of transgenic crops in most countries.

The Government of India is following a case-by-case approval of transgenic crops. Bt cotton is the first and only transgenic crop approved in India for commercial cultivation by the Genetic Engineering Approval Committee. The GEAC has also granted approval for large-scale fields trails for mustard by Pro-Agro Seed Company in 2001-02.

In 2003, Bt cotton covered an area of over two lakhs which is three times the coverage in 2002. The performance of Bt cotton versus the non-transgenic crop is being evaluated by the Ministry of Agriculture, Department of Biotechnology.

Public protest against GM crops indicates a divide between experts and lay perceptions of risk and uncertainty. India has expertise in safe production, use and handling of GM crops through its vast network of public and private institutions along with trained manpower. The country has well developed information sharing systems on environment, health agriculture and biotechnology sectors. However there is a need to develop integrated information systems through networking of institutions and database and to establish a biosafety-clearing house that would cover all information on transboundary inventories of GMO. To achieve this, extensive efforts have been made towards capacity building and currently FAO Regional Capacity Building Project on Biosafety of GM Crops in Asia and a GEF World Bank aided Capacity building are under implementation.

India has strongly opposed human cloning as it is unethical, but supports research on stem cells as they could be used to fight certain diseases.

Biotechnology has also been proposed to clone the Asiatic cheetah that vanished from India half a century ago. This attempt has been made by a laboratory—the Center for Cellular and Molecular Biology in Hyderabad that aims to use reproductive science to save endangered species. 1 The last record of the big cats was in 1948 when three cheetahs were shot by a Maharaja. Now only 300 are left. The big cats were thought to be beyond saving as they are descendents from a few dozen individuals and are therefore vulnerable to diseases.

Indian scientists at over ten institutions are working on the controversial 'terminator gene', i.e. crops that do not germinate for getting second crop through the seeds of the first one that bear the hitherto controversial gene called `terminator' gene. Funding for the research is from the Department of Biotechnology under the Ministry of Science and Technology. Farmers will now be able to get 'tailor-made crops', yield good crops and improve their harvests.

3.5.2 Robotics and Artificial intelligence

India plans to utilize a robot to assist astronauts during the lunar mission 2011. The researchers at the Indian Institute of Technology Kanpur have created a two-legged robot with camera and laser sensors called SmartNav. The Indian Space Research Organisation

1 National Post, 18 October 2000.

(ISRO) has shown interest in using a robot to assist astronauts in data gathering during Chandrayan-II Moon Mission in 2011.

India is awakening to the role of Robots in industry to increase productivity and quality. With the boom in the manufacturing sector, the robotics industry is gearing up for sharp growth in the non-governmental private sector too. At India's biggest auto manufacturer, Tata Motors, the employee strength has come down by 20 percent, while the company's turnover has increased 2 1/2 times. Its Pune plant alone has invested in 100 robots and the automaker is adding more. Sale of industrial robots is gathering pace in India as automobile companies expand their operations in the country. ABB has sold about 300 robots in India in the last seven years and expects double-digit growth in future. This has prompted ABB—one of the top three global manufacturers of robots—to consider setting up a manufacturing center in the country. With a cost advantage, owing to lower engineering costs in India, the country can produce more robots. Companies such as Precision Automation & Robotics (PARI) are already pitching its robots to large organizations in the United States and Europe. KUKA is one of the world leaders in providing engineering services and manufacturer of industrial robots has also entered the Indian market.

In an effort to develop robotics and automation that could end the almost complete dependence on imports of robotic arms in industrial manufacturing, young Indian scientists have developed a 'pick and place robot' (PP robot) as part of the "Home Grown Technology Program," on the initiative of Technology Information, Forecasting and Assessment Council (TIFAC), under the Department of Science and Technology (DST). India is thus emerging as the hub for industrial robots. At the same time, some companies are also developing robots that can clean homes and keep their homes safe -as developed by an Ahemdabad-based Gird Bot launching Robograd in January 2008. The robot, priced Rs 10,000, would roll out across India about a month. The company is hoping that the robot will also find an international market for its price and utility. But a bulk of India's robotics business is industrial, and that's growing because companies across the world want to reduce costs

In the field of medicine, the Department of Urology at the AIIMS recently performed the first Robotic Surgery in Asia. The procedure was performed with the help of the da Vinci S Robotic Surgical System, which is a state of the art four arms Robotic Surgical System and first such system in Asia. AIIMS pioneered this surgery in India and is the only center in the country performing this surgery routinely. It has now completed the first series of such surgeries in India and its availability within this country will prove a boon for the large Indian population.

3.5.3 Information Technology

Information Technology in India has followed two distinct paths-private owned network and state owned networks. The spread of connectivity by both these networks have been modest. While state owned network provides 50% of the connections available, the level of connectivity has been low as compared to other nations. The Ministry of Communication and Information Technology has set targets to improve high bandwidth broadband connectivity. BSNL has modified the broadband connectivity from 256 kilobytes to 2 megabytes per second download speed. This was easily accommodated as India has an installed bandwidth capacity of 16 terabits of which only 0.2 terabits have been used. 7

The Department of Telecommunications has decided to invest resources from the Universal Service Obligation Fund (USOF) in broadband technologies such as WiFi and WiMax. It is also planned to set up 8000 towers in remote areas that are presently not served by any telecom network. In order to achieve the broadband targets the Department of telecommunication has encouraged the local governments to implement their own wireless projects. Different states have evolved their own different connectivity models. One of the models worth a mention is the Akshaya Model in Kerala. The Akshaya telecenters use both wireless and wired networks and connectivity is provided through a public-private partnership. The project is expected to be expanded to the remaining 13 districts using the State Wide Area Network (SWAN) that has connectivity up to the block/sub-district level. SWAN is the core infrastructure developed by the Central Government under the National e-Governance Plan. It promises to offer e-government services and serve as a platform for government-to–government communication. Currently four states have the plan on schedule; certain states have an already existing network provided by National Informatics Center. The aim therefore is to synergise SWAN and avoid duplication.

The Department of Information Technology has launched a programme under its National e-Governance Plan to establish 100,000 telecenters. Currently there are about 12,000 to 13,000 telecenters across the country called Community Service Centers (CSC). Each CSC will serve five to six villages. The connectivity will be provided by SWAN and the content will be provided by various public sector agencies. These CSC's are managed and serviced by entrepreneurs and guided by services center agency that are often private agencies. In an attempt to make them accountable and serve the larger and social and development objectives, the lesson from Akshaya can prove to be useful. The public private partnership is run by a village entrepreneur but is accountable to the gram panchayat. The panchayat involvement is very high and the entrepreneur is only a catalyst. The ultimate beneficiaries are the people. The content is in the local language in agriculture, health and education. Another initiative is the e-seva in the west Godavari district of Andhra Pradesh where information related to various welfare schemes even to the village level has been put on the internet that can be accessed by the villagers at the community telecenters.

ICT industry is a major employer and revenue earner; therefore many state governments have not openly supported Free and Open Source Software for the fear of antagonizing the industry. Although the Indian government does not have any formal policy on FOSS, it is however supported in many ways. A National Resource Center for Free and Open Software has been created at Chennai and similar centers in Mumbai. The governments departments also encourage FOSS. The Electronics Corporation of Tamil Nadu –the ICT of the government supports FOSS. The government of Kerala has mandated the use of FOSS in schools.

The Indian IT industry (comprising the IT, ITES24 and hardware sectors) has been the "poster boy" of the entire liberalisation process. India's IT-ITES industry is expected to exceed USD 36 billion in annual revenue in the 2005-2006 financial years, and its contribution to the national GDP has been pegged at 4.8% for the same period. The total direct employment in the Indian IT-ITES sector is estimated to have grown by over a million, from 284,000 in the 1999-2000 period to a projected 1,287,000 in the past fiscal year (2005-2006). It is also estimated that the IT industry has helped create an additional three million job opportunities through indirect and induced employment (NASSCOM, 2006). India has developed considerable expertise in the software sector and is considered to as a world leader in software skilled professionals.

Investment in the IT sector has been encouraged in the sector through the Software Technology Parks Act and its liberal tax exemptions. The law provides direct and indirect tax exemptions as well as channels all relevant government licensing and permissions through a single agency.

3.5.4 Nanotechnology

India is a late entrant in the nanotechnology and with a small pool of skilled scientists and negligible interest from the industry; India has a long way to go before this technology can be used to solve its problem. Although there is support at the high scientific level, funding for the research is poor. India launched its nano Science and technology initiative in only 2008. Up to 2006, about US$ 24 million have been spend under the initiative.

Besides launching the Nano Science and Technology Initiative, India has also entered into bilateral nanotechnology programmes with the European Union, Germany, Italy, Taiwan and the United

States. In 2004, a National Center for Nanomaterials was set up at the International Advanced Research Center for Powder Metallurgy and New Materials (ARCI) in Hyderabad, in collaboration with Germany, Japan, Russia, Ukraine and the United States. When fully operational — possibly within about a year — the center will include pilot-scale facilities for producing and manipulating carbon nanotubes, ceramic and polymer composites reinforced with such nanotubes and nanopowders for water and air purification technologies. Four products from ARCI have already been transferred to the industry, including a water filter system for rural areas that uses silver nanoparticles and has shown good results. The center has also developed technology for coating materials with nanopowders.

Nanotechnology has also found uses in the field of medicine in India. The country has the highest estimated number of tuberculosis cases in the world and research is underway for the role of nanotechnology in this regard. A nano based TB diagnostic kit has been designed by the Central Scientific Instruments Organisation. The device does not require skilled technicians for its use and offers efficiency, user friendliness and is available for less than Rs. 30.

In January 2008, India formed the Vision Group to develop a national nanotechnology policy consisting of researchers from academia, industry and research. The Vision Group will be headed by C.N.R. Rao, nanotechnology researcher, national research professor, and chairman of India's Science Advisory Council. India has established several nanotechnology programs under its five-year nanotechnology initiative. The government recently announced a $250 million program that includes three national institutes for nanoscience. Two centers of excellence in nanotechnology are being set up here and in Mumbai with fabrication capabilities.

3.5 LINKAGES

The rate of inflation in India reached a 13-year high to 11.89% in

2008. The industrial growth and the employment created thereby has exerted huge pressures on the inflation and pushed it further up. The main cause is the increase in fuel price and its cascading effect on other food commodities and manufactured products. According to T.K. Arun in Economic Times, 10 April 2008, the diversion of corn for biofuel has sent the prices of other substitute grains and poultry soaring. This should be considered as a part of change in structural demand induced by the higher price of oil, which in turn is a result of higher growth in the emerging markets.

The unemployment rate of India has been decreasing steadily – according to The World Fact Book. In 2003 it was 8.8% ranked at 110, in the next year it rose to 9.5% thereafter decreasing to 7.2% in 2008 and improving the rank to 86th.

India is an agrarian economy. Although the industrial sector is growing at a phenomenal rate, a major section of the population is still engaged in agriculture and its allied activities. The country is self sufficient in food requirements for now. However, the rate of population growth far exceeds the rate of production and there will very soon be a need to depend on the outside market for food supply.

When the country first faced a food shortage in the 1960's-India adopted the Green Revolution. The scientists developed high yielding varieties to overcome the shortages and greatly increased the food grain production. The time for the second revolution is fast approaching. Genetic engineering in India has farmers already planting Bt cotton; the other GM crops are to be approved by the government.

Robotics and artificial intelligence in India has a long way to go. Robots in the industry can save on the labour used and thus save on the costs incurred. Many companies have realized the benefits of robotic automation in increasing the labour productivity.

In case of information and communication technology, India has emerged as a world leader in providing software solutions all over the world. India has clearly taken advantage of the low wage; English speaking highly educated technical labour to become the major destination for IT related services. The same trend is observed for other services like drug clinical trials and health care. India is emerging as a favourite destination for medical tourism for its health services of world standard and its low costs. Although the immediate effects of these services on employment may be limited, in the medium and long run, it would help in transforming the society.

Nanotechnology has various implications for the Indian society. From using nanoparticles to clean up its rivers and reduce pollution, to detecting Tuberculosis- plenty of Research and Development is required along with the support of industrial and the government sectors.

4 CHINA

Capital	— Beijing
Area	— 9,596,960 sq. km
Population	— 1,330,044,544 (July 2008 estimate)
Average rate of growth of population	— 0.629 %
Currency	— Renminbi (RMB) also referred to by the unit yuan (CNY)
GDP(PPP)	— $ 7.099 trillion(2007)
GDP (per capita PPP)	— $ 5,400 (2007)
GDP real growth rate	— 11.9 % (2007)
Agriculture as a share of GDP	— 11.3 % (2007)
Exports	— $1.22 trillion (2007)

Life Expectancy at birth	— 73.18 years (2008)
Infant mortality rate	— 21.16 deaths/1000 live birth (2008 est.)
Literacy	— 90.9% (2000 Census)
Human Development Index	— 0.777 ranked 81st

China is situated in the eastern part of Asia. The country is the second largest country in Asia and the third or fourth largest in the world. The uncertainty over size is due to territorial disputes. According to the World Fact Book, the area is 9,826,630 km^2 and the Encyclopedia Britannica claims China has an area of 9,522,055 km^2. The territory of People's Republic of China covers a large variety of landscapes. In the east, there are extensive densely populated alluvial plains, southern China is covered by hills and low mountain ranges and the west has major mountain ranges of the Himalayas and more arid landscape like the Taklamakan and the Gopi Desert.

China is considered to be an emerging superpower and is one of the fastest growing economies of the world. The country has recorded an average GDP of 9.4% for the past 25 years. Since 1978, China's market based reforms have helped to lift over 400 million Chinese people out of poverty- thus bringing the poverty rate from 53% of the population in 1981 to 8% in 2001.However, China is facing the problem of environmental damages as a price to pay for its development process. The continued expansion of deserts, especially the Gopi desert, carbon gases emission and water pollution. Leading Chinese environmentalist Ma Jun claims that drinking water of 300 million peasants is unsafe and water quality of one fifth of the cities is not up to the standard.

China has a population of 1.3 billion and has implemented a strict family policy. The government's goal is one child per family with exceptions for ethnic minorities and special cases. The aim is to stabilize population growth early in the 21st century and plan to continue with its policy till at least 2018. The policy is resisted in the rural area due to the need for agricultural labour and the traditional preference for sons. The decreasing reliability of the Census data has made the effectiveness of the policy difficult to determine. There are also concerns about the large imbalances in sex ratio at birth.

One of the major concerns of China is the issue of Human Rights. China is known in the international community for not having many rights and routinely violates international laws in human rights. Although the Constitution guarantees its citizens freedom of speech, freedom of press, the right to a fair trail, freedom of religion and property rights; censorship of political speeches and information is openly and routinely used to "protect national security interests". Press control is very tight. There have been widespread allegations of human rights violations including long detentions without trial, torture, restrictions on freedom of speech, religion and so on. China leads the world in capital punishments accounting for about 90% of the total executions in 2004. Human rights issue is one of the factors guiding the independence movements in Tibet and Xinjiang.

4.1 BRIEF HISTORY

The Chinese civilization is one of the oldest civilizations of the world dating back to about six millennia. It is the source of major inventions such as the paper, compass, printing and gunpowder. Joseph Needham, a British scholar calls them the Four Great inventions of Ancient China.

The last Civil War of China has resulted in two political states using the name China- the People's Republic of China (PRC) commonly known as China which consist of mainland China, Hong Kong and Macau and the Republic of China (ROC) commonly known as Taiwan that controls Taiwan and its surrounding islands.

The feudal states of the region were first united under Emperor Ch'in Shih Huang Ti. It was during his reign (246-210 BC) that work on the Great Wall of China had begun. Although the monument was meant to keep foreigners away, under the Han dynasty, extensive trade with the west was conducted. The subsequent dynasties- the Tang and the Song dynasty are consider the golden period of Chinese civilization. Chinese culture and technology reached its zenith during their reign. The Song dynasty was the first in world history to issue paper money and the first to have a permanent standing navy.

The Qing was the last dynasty in China, lasting till 1912. As China opened up to trade and missionary activities, opium produced in British India entered the country. Subsequent wars with Britain further weakened the Empire. Many uprising such as the Taiping Civil War (1851-1862), the Punti- Hakka Clan Wars (1855-1877), Nein Rebellion (1851-1868), Muslim Rebellion (1862-1877), Panthay Rebellion (1856-1873) and the Miao Rebellion (1854-1873) resulted in the loss of several million lives for each rebellion. Meanwhile Japan was rapidly modernizing its military and helped Korea to declare its independence. This led to the first Sino-Japanese war that resulted in China's cession of both Korea and Taiwan to Japan. Following this defeat Emperor Guangxu drafted a reform plan to make China a modern and Meji-style monarchy but was opposed and placed under house arrest by Empress Dowger Cixi. Further destruction followed in the form of the Boxer uprising.

The Boxer uprising was an attempt by a Chinese secret society to clear China of the foreigners and their influences from the country. The secret society (an offshoot of the Eight Trigrams Society) was called the I- ho Ch'uan which literally means righteous and harmonious fists. Translators trying to express this name came up with *Boxers.* When anti-foreign elements in Qing government won control in 1898, the Boxers joined them in driving out the foreigners. Thus the Boxer rebellion was not against the government but entirely against the foreigners. The Boxers resented the missionaries as well. In 1899, the missionaries and Chinese Christians came under attack. The Boxers besieged them in an enclave where the missionaries had set up defenses. An expeditionary force of European and Japanese troops came to help the besieged foreigners. However the Empress ordered all foreigners to be killed. In 1900, a second larger force captured Beijing and ended the Boxer rebellion. In 1901, a settlement was reached where the Empire government would pay reparations to the foreign governments.

By early 20th century, the people demanded reforms and mass civil disorder began. The 38 yr old Emperor Guangxu died under house arrest, just a day before Empress Cixi in 1908. He was succeeded by his 2 yr old nephew Puyi. Guangxu's consort became Empress Longyu and signed the abdication decree in 1912, thus ending two thousand years of imperial rule in China.

4.2 REPUBLIC OF CHINA

The Republic of China was established on January 1, 1912 with Sun-Yat sen of the Kuomintang (KMT or the nationalist Party) as the provisional president. Later the presidency was given to Yuan Shikai, a former Qing general who had ensured the defection of the entire Beijing army to the revolution. After his death in 1916, China was politically fragmented with a weak central government in Peking (Beijing). In the late 1920's under Chiang Kai-shek's leadership, the Kuomintang was able to unify all the fragments of the country and implemented the 'political tutelage'-an intermediate stage of political development in Sun Yat-sen's programme to make China a modern democratic state. Effectively it meant the rule of one party.

The Sino-Japanese War (1937-1945 a part of the World War II) forced an uneasy alliance between the Nationalists and the Communists. With the surrender of Japan in 1945, China emerged victorious but financially drained. The continued distrust between the Nationalists and Communists lead to the resumption of Chinese Civil War. In 1947, constitutional rule was established. After their victory in the Chinese Civil War, the Communist Party led by Mao Zedong, gained control of China. On October 1, 1949, the People's Republic of China was established. Beginning in 1970's the Republic of China began the implementation of full, multi-party, representative democracy in the territories still under its control.

After the Chinese Civil War, mainland China underwent a series of disruptive socioeconomic movements starting in the late 1950s with the Great Leap Forward and continued in the 1960s with the Cultural Revolution that left much of its education system and economy in shambles.

The Great Leap Forward (1958-1960). The Great Leap Forward began out of the conviction that China would have to industrialize on its own, without any outside help. It included various programmes such as rural collectivization, elimination of wage incentive and backyard steel plants. However the programme only led to the death of 15-30 million people and plunged China into economic depression in the early 1960's.

Mao called for the peasants to be organized into communes at the village and country wide level. He also called for peasants to build backyard furnaces to make useful iron and steel tools from scrap metals. In order to fulfill the quotas, however the peasants began to melt down useful equipments. The consequence was that labour was moved away from food production leading to a shortfall in output. Due to the highly centralized system, this shortfall was not reported on time. A severe famine followed that killed 15-30 million people; the exact figure of starvation deaths are yet unknown.

When Mao finally accepted that the Great Leap Forward was a failure, he left the process of economic recovery to Deng Xiaoping, Liu Shaoqi and Zhou Enlai. Under the new leadership there was a shift to expertise rather than ideological purity. In 1966, Mao sought to return to power. The struggle took the form of the Great Proletarian Cultural Revolution.

The Great Proletarian Cultural Revolution (1966-1976) Although the Cultural Revolution was a disaster for China it was a brilliant piece of guerilla action on Mao's part in the power struggle he instigated. Mao launched the Cultural Revolution in August of 1966 at a Plenum of the Central Committee when he called for Red Guards to challenge Communist Party officials for their bourgeois-ness and lack of revolutionary zeal. Schools were closed to free students to join the Red Guards. The turmoil and disruptions of the Cultural Revolution led to a decline in industrial production of 12 % between 1966 and 1968.

Following Zhou's death on January 8, 1976, his successor, Vice Premier Deng Xiaoping, was supplanted within a month by Hua Guofeng, former minister of public security. Hua became permanent premier in April. In October, he was named successor to Mao as chairman of the Communist Party. But Mao's death on September 10th unleashed the bitter rivalries within the party that had been suppressed since the Cultural Revolution. Old opponents of Mao launched a campaign against his widow, Jiang Qing, and three of her "radical" colleagues. The so-called Gang of Four was denounced for having undermined the party, the government, and the economy. They were tried and convicted in 1981. Meanwhile, in 1977, Deng Xiaoping was reinstated as deputy premier.

In 1981, Deng protégé Hu Yaobang replaced Hua Guofeng as party chairman. Deng became chairman of the Central Committee's military commission, giving him control over the army. The body's 215 members concluded the session with a statement holding Mao Zedong responsible for the "grave blunder" of the Cultural Revolution.

Under Deng Xiaoping's leadership, meanwhile, China's Communist ideology went through a massive reinterpretation, and sweeping economic changes were set in motion in the early 1980s. The Chinese scrapped the personality cult that idolized Mao Zedong, muted Mao's old call for class struggle and exportation of the Communist revolution, and imported Western technology and management techniques to replace the Marxist tenets that had slowed modernization.

The Tiananmen incident: The removal of Hu Yaobang as party chairman in January 1987 signaled a hard-line resurgence within the party. The death of Hu Yaobang on April 15, 1989, coupled with growing economic hardship caused by high inflation, provided the backdrop for a large-scale protest movement by students, intellectuals, and other parts of a disaffected urban population. University students and other citizens camped out in Beijing's Tiananmen Square to mourn Hu's death and to protest against those who would slow reform. Their protests, which grew despite government efforts to contain them, called for an end to official corruption and for defense of freedoms guaranteed by the Chinese constitution. Protests also spread too many other cities, including Shanghai, Chengdu, and Guangzhou.

Martial law was declared on May 20, 1989. Late on June 3rd and early on the morning of June 4th, military units were brought into Beijing. They used armed force to clear demonstrators from the streets. There are no official estimates of deaths in Beijing, but most observers believe that casualties numbered in the hundreds.

After June 4, while foreign governments expressed horror at the brutal suppression of the demonstrators, the central government eliminated remaining sources of organized opposition, detained large numbers of protesters, and required political reeducation not only for students but also for large numbers of party cadre and government officials. Following the resurgence of conservatives in the aftermath of June 4, economic reform slowed until given new impetus by Deng Xiaoping's dramatic visit to southern China in early 1992.

After Zhao became the party General Secretary, the economic and political reforms he had championed came under increasing attack. His proposal in May 1988 to accelerate price reform led to widespread popular complaints about rampant inflation and gave opponents of rapid reform the opening to call for greater centralization of economic controls and stricter prohibitions against Western influence. This precipitated a political debate, which grew more heated through the winter of 1988-89.

In annual sessions of the rubber-stamp National People's Congress in 1992 and 1993, the government called for accelerating the drive for economic reform, but the sessions were widely seen as an effort to maintain China's moves toward a market economy while retaining political authoritarianism. At the session in 1993, Communist Party leader Jiang Zemin was elected president, while hard-liner Li Peng was reelected to another five-year term as prime minister. Since 1993, the Chinese economy has continued to grow rapidly.

Third Generation of Leader: Deng's health deteriorated in the years prior to his death in 1997. During that time, President

Jiang Zemin and other members of his generation gradually assumed control of the day-to-day functions of government. This "third generation" leadership governed collectively with President Jiang at the center. In March 1998, Jiang was re-elected President during the 9th National People's Congress. In 1998, Premier Zhu Rongji introduced a sweeping program to privatize state-run businesses and further liberalize the nation's economy, a move lauded by Western economists. On July 1, 1997, when Britain's lease on the New Territories expired, Hong Kong returned to Chinese sovereignty, and in 1999, the Portuguese colony of Macao also was returned to Chinese rule.

China was admitted to the World Trade Organization in November 2001. Its entry ended a 15-year debate over whether China is entitled to the full trading rights of capitalist countries.

Fourth Generation of Leaders: In November 2002, Vice President Hu Jintao became general secretary of the Communist Party at the 16th Party Congress, succeeding President Jiang. Hu Jintao also assumed the presidency in March 2003.

Tension between China and Taiwan intensified in March 2005, when China passed an anti-secession law that said the country could use force if Taiwan moved toward achieving independence. The legislation stated that the state should employ non-peaceful means if necessary to protect China's sovereignty and territorial integrity. The Taiwan president called the bill a "law of aggression".

In May 2006, China completed construction on the Three Gorges Dam, the largest hydroelectric dam in the world. More than a million people will be displaced when the area is flooded. In July 2006, China opened a $4.2-billion, 710-mile-long railway from Qinghai Province to the Tibetan capital of Lhasa. The highest railway in the world, it ascends as high as 16,500 ft, requiring all compartments to have regulated oxygen levels. The railway will increase ethnic Chinese migration into Tibet, which many see as a deliberate attempt to dilute Tibetan culture.

In the spring and summer of 2007, dog food and toothpaste products that originated in China were recalled due to the presence of poisonous ingredients, leading many to question the safety of Chinese products and the reliability of its regulatory system. In July, China's former head of the State Food and Drug Administration was executed for accepting bribes from pharmaceutical companies in exchange for favors.

China is firmly committed to economic reform and opening to the outside world. The Chinese leadership has identified reform of state industries and the establishment of a social safety net as government priorities. Government strategies for achieving these goals include large-scale privatization of unprofitable state-owned enterprises and development of a pension system for workers. The leadership has also downsized the government bureaucracy. The coming years represents a crucial period in China's development. To investors and firms, the country is a vast market that has yet to be tapped and is a low cost base for export-oriented production.

The next few years represent a critical period in China's development. To investors and firms, especially following China's accession to the World Trade Organization (WTO) in 2001, China represents a vast market that has yet to be fully tapped and a low-cost base for export-oriented production. Educationally, China is forging ahead as partnerships and exchanges with foreign universities have helped create new research opportunities for its students. China hosted the Summer Olympics in 2008 and this event was used as an opportunity to showcase China's development gains of the past two decades. The new leadership is committed to generating greater economic development in the interior and providing more services to those who do not live in China's coastal areas, goals that form the core of President Hu's concepts of a "harmonious society" and a "spiritual civilization." However, there is still much that needs to change in China. Human rights issues remain a major concern, as does China's lack of effective controls to prevent proliferation of weapons of mass destruction (WMD)-related materials and technology. Abatement of pollution and improvements in systems to ensure food, drug, and product safety are issues on which the United States has begun work with China.

4.3 GOVERNMENT AND POLITICS

The Chinese Communist Party, authoritarian in structure and ideology, continues to dominate government. Nevertheless, China's population, geographical vastness, and social diversity frustrate attempts to rule by fiat from Beijing. Central leaders must increasingly build consensus for new policies among party members, local and regional leaders, influential non-party members, and the population at large.

In periods of greater openness, the influence of people and organizations outside the formal party structure has tended to increase, particularly in the economic realm. This phenomenon is most apparent today in the rapidly developing coastal region. Nevertheless, in all-important government, economic and cultural institutions in China, party committees work to see that party and state policy guidance is followed and that non-party members do not create autonomous organizations that could challenge party rule. Party control is tightest in government offices and in urban economic, industrial, and cultural settings; it is considerably looser in the rural areas, where the majority of the people live.

Theoretically, the party's highest body is the Party Congress, which traditionally meets at least once every 5 years. The 17th Party Congress took place in fall 2007. The primary organs of power in the Communist Party include:

- The Politburo Standing Committee, which currently consists of nine members;
- The Politburo, consisting of 24 full members, including the members of the Politburo Standing Committee;
- The Secretariat, the principal administrative mechanism of the CCP, headed by the General Secretary;
- The Central Military Commission;
- The Discipline Inspection Commission, which is charged with rooting out corruption and malfeasance among party cadres.

4.3.1 State Structure

The Chinese Government has always been subordinate to the Chinese Communist Party (CCP); its role is to implement party policies. The primary organs of state power are the National People's Congress (NPC), the President (the head of state), and the State Council. Members of the State Council include Premier Wen Jiabao (the head of government), a variable number of vice premiers (now four), five state councilors (protocol equivalents of vice premiers but with narrower portfolios), and 22 ministers and four State Council commission directors.

Under the Chinese constitution, the NPC is the highest organ of state power in China. It meets annually for about 2 weeks to review and approve major new policy directions, laws, the budget, and major personnel changes. When the NPC is not in session, its permanent organ, the Standing Committee, exercises state power

4.3.2 Legal System

The government's efforts to promote rule of law are significant and ongoing. After the Cultural Revolution, China's leaders aimed to develop a legal system to restrain abuses of official authority and revolutionary excesses. In 1982, the National People's Congress adopted a new state constitution that emphasized the rule of law under which even party leaders are theoretically held accountable.

Since 1979, when the drive to establish a functioning legal system began, more than 300 laws and regulations, most of them in the economic area, have been promulgated. An innovative device was the use of mediation committees—informed groups of citizens who resolve about 90% of China's civil disputes and some minor criminal cases at no cost to the parties. There are more than 800,000 such committees in both rural and urban areas.

Legal reform became a government priority in the 1990s. Legislation designed to modernize and professionalize the nation's lawyers, judges, and prisons was enacted. The 1994 Administrative Procedure Law allows citizens to sue officials for abuse of authority or malfeasance. In addition, the criminal law and the criminal procedures laws were amended to introduce significant reforms. The criminal law amendments abolished the crime of "counter-revolutionary" activity, although many persons are still incarcerated for that crime. Criminal procedures reforms also encouraged establishment of a more transparent, adversarial trial process. The Chinese constitution and laws provide for fundamental human rights, including due process, but these are often ignored in practice. In addition to other judicial reforms, the Constitution was amended in 2004 to include the protection of individual human rights and legally obtained private property, but it is unclear how those provisions will be implemented. Although new criminal and civil laws have provided additional safeguards to citizens, previously debated political reforms, including expanding elections to the township level, and other legal reforms, including the reform of the reeducation through labor system, have been put on hold.

China and Taiwan: The island of Taiwan and the surrounding islands are administered by the Republic of China – a democratic multi-party state. After the founding of the People's Republic in1949, both Taiwan and China claimed to be the sole legitimate ruler of "China". After the Kuomintang retreat to Taiwan in 1949, the Republic of China (ROC) had maintained official relations with most states of the world. However by the 1970's, a shift in the international diplomatic relations gave the People's Republic of China (PRC) an upper hand in international relations and recognition.

Under resolution 2758, the representatives of Chiang Kai-shek to the United Nations were expelled in 1971 and the representatives of the People's Republic of China were invited to assume China's seat. Later attempts by the republic of China to rejoin the UN have been blocked by the People's Republic of China or rejected by the UN. Due to the fact that most international organizations observe the One China Policy of the People's Republic of China, the PRC has been able to presurrise organizations such as WHO to refuse official recognition to POC.

Since its retreat to Taiwan, the ROC has not formally renounced its claim to all of China, nor has it changed its official maps, which includes the mainland and Mongolia. Following the introduction to full democracy and the electoral victory of DPP's Chen Shui-bian in the presidential elections, the Republic of China has not pursued its claims on the mainland and in Mongolia. The current DPP Administration has adopted a policy of separating the state's identity from "China", while moving towards identifying the state as "Taiwan". The ROC has not made formal moves to change the name, flag, or national anthem of the state to reflect a Taiwan identity due to pressure from the United States and the fear of invasion or military action from the People's Republic of China against the island. The People's Republic of China claims to have succeeded the Republic of China as the sole legitimate governing authority of all of China, which, from the official viewpoint of People's Republic of China, includes the island of Taiwan.

4.4 ECONOMY

China has opened its economy since 1979. The Chinese leadership has adopted a more pragmatic approach and has reduced the role of ideology in economic policy. The market-oriented reforms that the country had implemented have unleashed individual initiative and entrepreneurship. The result has been the largest reduction of poverty and one of the fastest increases in income levels ever seen.

In the 1980's China combined central planning with market-oriented reforms to increase productivity and technological quality. China also undertook agricultural reforms by dismantling the commune system and introducing a household based system that gave peasants more decision-making abilities. Non-agricultural activities in the rural areas like village enterprises were also encouraged. These reforms lead to an average annual rate of growth of 10% in agriculture and industrial output. The country became self sufficient in grain production. The rural economy accounted for 23% of agricultural output –this helped to absorb the surplus labour in the countryside. However by the late 1980's the economy became overheated with inflation. China gained her momentum again in the early 1990's. The 10-year development plan of the 1990's stressed continuity in the political system with more bold reforms of the economic system.

In October 2003, at the Third Plenum of the Chinese Communist Party, the legislators proposed several amendments to the state constitution. One of the important amendment was the protection of private property rights. The fifth Plenum in October 2005 approved the 11th Five Year economic Programme that aims at building a harmonious society through a balanced wealth distribution and improved education, medical care and social security.

4.4.1 Population

Initially, China's post-1949 leaders were ideologically disposed to view a large population as an asset. But the liabilities of a large, rapidly growing population soon became apparent. For one year, starting in August 1956, vigorous propaganda support was given to the Ministry of Public Health's mass birth control efforts. These efforts, however, had little impact on fertility. After the interval of the Great Leap Forward, Chinese leaders again saw rapid population growth as an obstacle to development, and their interest in birth control revived. The chaos of the Cultural Revolution however, brought the program to a halt. Population growth targets were set for both administrative units and individual families. In the mid-1970s the maximum recommended family size was two children in cities and three or four in the country. Since 1979 the government has advocated a one-child limit for both rural and urban areas and has generally set a maximum of two children in special circumstances. As of 1986 the policy for minority nationalities was two children per couple, three in special circumstances, and no limit for ethnic groups with very small populations. The one-child policy was a highly ambitious population control program. Like previous programs of the 1960s and 1970s, the one-child policy employed a combination of propaganda, social pressure, and in some cases coercion. The one-child policy was unique, however, in that it linked reproduction with economic cost or benefit.

Under the one-child program, a sophisticated system rewarded those who observed the policy and penalized those who did not. Couples with only one child were given a "one-child certificate" entitling them to such benefits as cash bonuses, longer maternity leave, better child care, and preferential housing assignments. In return, they were required to pledge that they would not have more children. In the countryside, there was great pressure to adhere to the one-child limit. Because the rural population accounted for approximately 60 % of the total, the effectiveness of the one-child policy in rural areas was considered the key to the success or failure of the program as a whole. The one-child policy enjoyed much greater success in urban than in rural areas. Even without state intervention, there were compelling reasons for urban couples to limit the family to a single child. Raising a child required a significant portion of family income, and in the cities a child did not become an economic asset until he or she entered the work force at age sixteen. Couples with only one child were given preferential treatment in housing allocation. In addition, because city dwellers who were employed in state enterprises received pensions after retirement, the sex of their first child was less important to them than it was to those in rural areas. As of 2007, the population of China was 1,321,851,888 with a growth rate of 0.606%. Life expectancy is 72.88 years- 74.82 yrs for females and 71.13 yrs for males. The literacy rate in the country is 90.9% with 86.5% literacy among the females and 95.1% among the males. The UN ranks China as 81st among the 117 countries ranked in the Human Development Index, and China thus falls in the medium category.

4.5 SECTORAL GROWTH

4.5.1 Agriculture

China is the world's most populous country and one of the largest producers and consumers of agricultural products. Roughly half of China's labor force is engaged in agriculture, even though only 10% of the land is suitable for cultivation and agriculture contributes only 13% of China's GDP. China's cropland area is only 75% of the U.S. total, but China still produces about 30% more crops and livestock than the United States. Because of intensive cultivation, China is among the world's largest producers of rice, corn, wheat, soybeans, vegetables, tea, and pork. Major non-food crops include cotton, other fibers, and oilseeds. China hopes to further increase agricultural production through improved plant stocks, fertilizers, and technology. Incomes for Chinese farmers are stagnating, leading to an increasing wealth gap between the cities and countryside. Government policies that continue to emphasize grain self-sufficiency and the fact that farmers do not own—and cannot buy or sell—the land they work, have contributed to this situation. In addition, inadequate port facilities and lack of warehousing and cold storage facilities impede both domestic and international agricultural trade.

Before the early 1980s, most of the agricultural sector was organized according to the three-tier commune system (cooperatives, collectives, communes). There were over 50,000 people's communes, most containing around 30,000 members. Each commune was made up of about sixteen production brigades, and each production brigade was composed of around seven production teams. The production teams were the basic agricultural collective units. They corresponded to small villages and typically included about 30 households and 100 to 250 members. The communes, brigades, and teams owned all major rural productive assets and provided nearly all administrative, social, and commercial services in the countryside. The largest part of farm family incomes consisted of shares of net team income, distributed to members according to the amount of work each had contributed to the collective effort. Farm families also worked small private plots and were free to sell or consume their products.

After 1978, decollectivization, price increases and the relaxation of trade restrictions on most agricultural products accompanied the take off of China's food economy. Between 1978 and 1984, grain production increased by 4.7 % per year; the output of fruit rose by 7.2 % (Table 1). The highest annual growth rates came in the oilseed, livestock and aquatic product sectors, sectors that expanded in real value terms by 14.9, 9.1 and 7.9 %, respectively.

Agricultural growth remained remarkable for most agricultural products from 1985 to 2000. Fishery production experienced the fastest growth from 1985 to 1995 (13.7 % annual growth, Table 1). Although its annual growth rate fell in the following period, it still recorded 10.2 % between 1996 and 2000. Over the same period, meat production and vegetable-sown areas expanded from 7 to 9 % annually. Other cash crops such as oil crops, soybean and fruits also grew at rates much higher than population growth.

Overall growth of the agriculture sector remained at the annual rate of 3.4 % from 2001 to 2004 and 1996 to 2000. Comparing the growth rates of individual commodities between these two periods, it appears that production (measured in quantity) growth of many individual agricultural commodities fell, which may indicate that China's agricultural production has been shifting from aggregate production to value-added and quality food production.

Table 4.1. The annual growth rates (%) of the agricultural economy, 1970–2004

	Pre-reform	Reform period			
	1970–1978	1979–1984	1985–1995	1996–2000	2001–2004
Agricultural GDP	2.7	7.1	4.0	3.4	3.4
Production:					
Grain	2.8	4.7	1.7	0.03	-0.2
Cotton	-0.4	19.3	-0.3	-1.9	6.5
Soybean	-2.3	5.2	2.8	2.6	2.4
Oil crops	2.1	14.9	4.4	5.6	0.6
Fruit	6.6	7.2	12.7	8.6	29.5
Meat	4.4	9.1	8.8	6.5	4.6
Fishery	5.0	7.9	13.7	10.2	3.5
Planted area:					
Vegetables	2.4	5.4	6.8	6.8	3.8
Orchards (fruit)	8.1	4.5	10.4	1.5	2.2

Sources: NSBC (1985–2005) and MOA (1985–2005).

Structural changes in agricultural production: By the end of 1984, approximately 98 % of the old production teams had adopted the contract responsibility system, and all but 249 communes had been dissolved, their governmental functions passed on to 91,000 township and town governments. Production team organizations were replaced by 940,000 village committees. Under the responsibility system, farm families no longer devoted most of their efforts to collective production but instead generally signed contracts with the village or town to cultivate a given crop on a particular piece of land. After harvest a certain amount of the crop had to be sold to the unit at a predetermined price, and any output beyond that amount was the property of the family, either to be sold in the market or to be consumed. Beyond the amount contracted for delivery to the collective, farmers were allowed to determine for themselves what and how to produce.

Market activity played a central role in the rural economy of the 1980s. Farmers sold a growing share of their produce in rural or urban free markets and purchased many of the inputs that had formerly been supplied by the team or brigade. A prominent new institution that thrived in the market environment was the "specialized household." Specialized households operated in the classic pattern of the entrepreneur, buying or renting equipment to produce a good or service that was in short supply locally. The new economic climate and the relaxation of restrictions on the movements of rural residents gave rise to numerous opportunities for profit-making ventures in the countryside. Towns, villages, and groups of households referred to as "rural economic unions" established small factories, processing operations, construction teams, catering services, and other kinds of nonagricultural concerns. Many of these organizations had links with urban enterprises that found the services of these rural units to be less expensive and more efficient than those of their formal urban counterparts. The growth of these nonagricultural enterprises in the countryside created a large number of new jobs, making it possible for many workers who were no longer needed in agriculture to "leave the land but stay in the country," significantly changing the structure of the rural economy and increasing rural incomes.

Although the chief characteristic of the new rural system was household farming for profit, collective organizations still played a major role. Agricultural land was still owned by township or town governments, which determined the crops farmers contracted to grow and the financial terms of the contracts. Many townships, towns, and village governments also engage in major entrepreneurial undertakings, establishing factories, processing mills, brick works, and other large-scale enterprises. Finally, the maintenance and operation of public works, such as irrigation systems, power plants, schools, and clinics, generally still was regarded as the responsibility of the collective administrations.

Thus, China's agriculture has undergone significant changes since the early 1980s. Rapid economic growth, urbanization and market development are key factors underlining the changes. Rising income and urban expansion have boosted the demand for meat, fruit and other non-staple foods. These changes have stimulated sharp shifts in the structure of agriculture. For example, the share of livestock output value rose 2.5 times from 14 % to 35 % between 1970 and 2004 (Table 2). Aquatic products increased at an even more rapid rate. One of the most significant signs of structural changes in the agriculture sector is that the share of crops in total agricultural output fell from 82 % in 1970 to 51 % in 2004.

Table 4.2. Changes in structure (%) of China's agricultural economy, 1970–2004

	1970	1980	1985	1990	1995	2000	2004
Share in agricultural output							
Crops	82	76	69	65	58	56	51
Livestock	14	18	22	26	30	30	35
Fishery	2	2	3	5	8	11	10
Forestry	2	4	5	4	3	4	4

Source: NSBC, *China's statistical yearbook*, various issues and *China rural statistical yearbook*, various issues.

Within the crop sector, the importance of the three major crops, rice, wheat and maize, has waxed and waned. The share of the major cereal grains increased from 50 % in 1970 to a peak level of 57 % in 1990 and then gradually declined to less that 50 % in 2004 (Table 3). Most of the fall has been due to diminishing rice- and wheat-sown areas. In contrast, the shares of maize areas grew by more than 50 % between 1970 and 2000 (Table 3). The rise in maize area, China's main feed grain, is correlated in no small way with the rapid expansion of the nation's livestock production during the same period.

Table 4.3. Shares of crop-sown areas, 1970–2004

	1970	1980	1985	1990	1995	2000	2004
Rice	22.1	23.1	21.9	22.3	20.5	19.2	18.5
Wheat	17.4	19.7	20.0	20.7	19.3	17.1	14.1
Maize	10.8	13.7	12.1	14.4	15.2	14.8	16.6
Soybean	5.5	4.9	5.3	5.1	5.4	6.0	6.2
Sweet potato	5.9	5.1	4.2	4.2	4.1	3.7	3.2
Cotton	3.4	3.4	3.5	3.8	3.6	2.6	3.7
Rapeseed	1.0	1.9	3.1	3.7	4.6	4.8	4.7
Peanut	1.2	1.6	2.3	2.0	2.5	3.1	3.1
Sugar crops	0.4	0.6	1.0	1.2	1.3	1.0	1.0
Tobacco	0.2	0.3	0.9	0.9	0.9	0.8	0.8
Vegetables	2.0	2.2	3.2	4.3	6.3	9.7	11.4
Others	30.1	23.5	22.5	17.4	16.3	17.2	16.7
Total	100.0	100.0	100.0	100.0	100.0	100.0	100.0

Source: NSBC, *China's statistical yearbook*, various issues; *China rural statistical yearbook*, various issues.

In addition to maize, other cash crops such as vegetables, edible oil crops, sugar crops and tobacco have expanded in area. In the 1970s, vegetables accounted for only about 2% of total crop area; by 2004, the share had increased by nearly six times (Table 3). The area devoted to edible oil also grew by two to three times. Field interviews reveal that the livelihood of the poor relies more on crops than livestock and fishery (when compared to richer farmers). Within the crop sector, poorer farmers produce more grains (particularly maize) than cash crops. These figures might imply that the poor have gained somewhat less than better off farmers from the diversification of agricultural production during the reform period.

Challenges ahead: Despite overall economic growth the urban-rural divide has remained high (3:1) To correct this disparity, the Chinese Eleventh Five Year Plan has included the "New Rural Development" programme, which intends to give rural development a higher priority. One of the immediate policy reforms is to abolish all fees and taxes associated with agricultural production. This is a very significant move because it is for the first in several thousand years that no tax and fees are imposed on peasants. This reflects the determination of the Chinese leadership to deal with rural backwardness.

4.5.2 Industry

Industry and construction account for about 49.5% of China's GDP (2007). In 1949, the Chinese government started large scaled, planned construction. As a result, the country's industrial foundation was strengthened and its production level rose rapidly. The metallurgical, mining and energy industries, airplane and automobile industries, and new industries, including petrochemicals, computers, telecommunication equipment, instruments and meters, and aeronautics have become the major industries of the country. Since 1978, the policies of reform and opening to the outside world have enabled China's industry to enter a stage of great innovation and development. From 1978 to 1999, China's industry grew at an average rate of 11.1 % every year, and the comprehensive industrial strength was remarkably enhanced. By 1999, some 3,535.7 billion Yuan of industrial added value had been attained; an increase of 10.2 times over 1978. China has become a preferred destination for the relocation of global manufacturing facilities. Its strength as an export platform has contributed to incomes and employment in China.

China's industrial reform first began by giving more rights and leaving more profits for enterprises, extending enterprises' independent operations and practicing the enterprise contract responsibility system. This fully mobilized the initiative and creativeness of enterprises, their workers and staff members, and created an excellent environment for the improvement of the operation mechanism of enterprises. China also increased industrialization through the introduction of foreign capital and opening to the outside world. The establishment of large numbers of Sino-foreign joint and wholly foreign-owned enterprises has not only brought more capital to enterprises, but also advanced equipment and modern management. Through more than two decades of reform, China's industry overcame the backwardness that only allowed it to make one or a few varieties of products because of its low technological level. The production level of industrial products has increased by a huge margin. In 1999, the outputs of steel, raw coal, electricity and cement were 124 million tons, 1.045 billion tons, 1,239.3 billion kWh and 573 million tons-increases of 3.9 times, 69 %, 4.8 and 8.8 times over 1978, respectively. The growth rates of chemical fibers, fertilizers, ethylene, plastics, plate glass and other important means of production products have doubled or more than doubled. Many consumer goods closely related to people's lives have grown from zero and expanded from small to large; the growth rate of some products has even reached more than one hundred times, such as color TV sets, refrigerators, washing machines, air-conditioners, cameras, video recorders, VCD and DVD sets, and stereos. The output of cars is also increasing at a rapid rate, along with the increasing number of cars possessed by households.

The state-owned sector still accounts for about 40% of GDP. The reform of state industrial enterprises, especially large and medium-sized enterprises, is the constant focus of China's economic system reform. While many small State Owned Enterprises (SOE) have been privatized, medium and large SOE's are mostly intact and receive generous subsidies. In recent years, authorities have been giving greater attention to the management of state assets—both in the financial market as well as among state-owned-enterprises—and progress has been noteworthy.

4.5.3 Foreign Investment

China's investment climate has changed dramatically since the reforms were introduced in 1979. China has become the second largest Foreign Direct Investment (FDI) recipient in the world, after the US and the largest host country among developing countries. In the early 1980s, China restricted foreign investments to export-oriented operations and required foreign investors to form joint-venture partnerships with Chinese firms. FDI grew quickly during the 1980s, but slowed in late 1989 in the aftermath of Tiananmen. In response, the government introduced legislation and regulations designed to encourage foreigners to invest in high-priority sectors and regions. Since the early 1990s, China has allowed foreign investors to manufacture and sell a wide range of goods on the domestic market, and authorized the establishment of wholly foreign-owned enterprises, now the preferred form of FDI. However, the Chinese Government's emphasis on guiding FDI into manufacturing has led to market saturation in some industries, while leaving China's services sectors underdeveloped.

As part of its WTO accession, China undertook to eliminate certain trade-related investment measures and to open up specified sectors that had previously been closed to foreign investment. New laws, regulations, and administrative measures to implement these commitments are being issued. Major remaining barriers to foreign investment include opaque and inconsistently enforced laws and regulations and the lack of a rules-based legal infrastructure.

Opening to the outside remains central to China's development. Foreign-invested enterprises produce about half of China's exports, and China continues to attract large investment inflows. Foreign exchange reserves were $1.066 trillion at the end of 2006, and have now surpassed those of Japan, making China's foreign exchange reserves the largest in the world.

Chinese FDI trends can be distinguished into three phases-first phase 1979-84 second phase-1984 91 and third phase 1992 onwards. In the first phase the Chinese government set up four Special Economic Zones and offered special incentives for FDI. While FDI into China was concentrated in these areas, the amount was limited. During these five years, FDI amounted to only US$ 1.8 billion. In the second phase, the coastal cities across ten provinces were opened and FDI's began to increase. Total FDI amounted to $ 10.3 billion in the period 1984- 89. However this decreased sharply in 989, mainly due to the Tiananmen incident. FDI slowed down to 2.8% in 1990. Even though the growth rate increased later on, for the period the overall rate lowered to 11%, which was much lower than the 38.1% growth rate during 1984-88. The third phase began in 1992 when the government adopted a new approach to move away from special regimes towards a nation wide implementation of open policies for FDI. The result was that in 1998 the FDI touched $ 45,463 million. According to the latest records, China's FDI in 2005 amounted to $72.5 billion, an increase of 19.42% from the year 2004. Measured on a purchasing power parity (PPP) basis, China in 2007 stood as the second-largest economy in the world after the US, although in per capita terms the country is still lower middle-income. Despite an increased backlash against foreign mergers and acquisitions, annual inflows of foreign direct investment in 2006 rose to $63 billion. By the end of 2006, more than 5,000 domestic Chinese enterprises had established direct investments in 172 countries and regions around the world.

The figures for outward FDI vary. According to China's BOP statistics, the cumulative total during 1990-97 was US$ 18.9 billion, consisting mainly of equity capital. Officially, the Chinese State Owned Enterprises had as many as 5,666 affiliates aboard at the end of 1998 with a combined FDI of $6.33 billion.

The Chinese government faces several economic development challenges: (a) to sustain adequate job growth for tens of millions of workers laid off from state-owned enterprises, migrants, and new entrants to the work force; (b) to reduce corruption and other economic crimes; and (c) to contain environmental damage and social strife related to the economy's rapid transformation. Economic development has been more rapid in coastal provinces than in the interior, and approximately 200 million rural laborers have relocated to urban areas to find work. One demographic consequence of the one child policy is that China is now one of the most rapidly aging countries in the world. Deterioration in the environment - notably air pollution, soil erosion, and the steady fall of the water table, especially in the north - is another long-term problem. China continues to lose arable land because of erosion and economic development. In 2007 China intensified government efforts to improve environmental conditions, tying the evaluation of local officials to environmental targets, publishing a national climate change policy, and establishing a high level leading group on climate change, headed by Premier WEN Jiabao. The Chinese government seeks to add energy production capacity from sources other than coal and oil as its double-digit economic growth increases demand. Chinese energy officials in 2007 agreed to purchase five third generation nuclear reactors from Western companies. More power generating capacity came on line in 2006 as large-scale investments - including the Three Gorges Dam across the Yangtze River - were completed.

4.6 EMERGING TECHNOLOGIES IN CHINA

4.6.1 Genetic Engineering

China has a tremendously rich genetic diversity evolved through thousands of years of evolution and cultivation. The country has developed a large germplasm pool from which scientists can choose the desired varieties. There are about 120,000 accessions of rice germplasmas in the world and about 80,000 are in China. Such richness in germplasma provides a good resource for genetic research. With the development of modern genetics, scientists have paid more attention to the genetic values of these varieties. Although rice genetic research lagged behind in the country, with the help of the resource advantages, the progress is catching up with the world scientific community. So far 16 mutant/variant genes including MOC1, BC1, SKC1 and Rf genes have been isolated and characterized by China.[1]

Rice is an important crop for the Chinese people feeding more than 60% of the people and providing about 40% of the calorie intake. Hybrid rice has greatly contributed to the self –sufficiency of food in China. To ensure fôod security for the increasing population, increasing the yield ceiling remains a priority in China. Based on the per capita rice consumption of 150 kg and a stable rice cropping area of 31.57 million hmz, the rice yield should be increased to $6.885 x 10^3$ and $7.845 x 10^3$ kg per hmz in 2010 and 2030 respectively. Based on the experiences of high yielding rice breeding in China and the new plant type rice breeding at the international Rice Research Institute, a special Collaborative research programme on super rice breeding was established by the Ministry of Agriculture, China in 1996. Under good management the hybrid has been producing high yields. So far the Ministry of Agriculture of China has released 35 super hybrids for production. It is estimated that these super hybrid were planted in total area of 13.5 million hmz and produced 6.7 thousand million kg rice in 1998-2005.[2]

The most important gene resource in rice genetics and breeding in the world is the semi-dwarf gene SD1. The exploitation and use of semi-dwarf in 1960's led to the great achievement that was widely known as the Green Revolution stimulated a major increase in rice production in China. In China, the first rice transgenic plant produced by Baojian Li in 1990. Since then transgenic rice plants have been produced. The first transgenic hybrid rice with an herbicide tolerance gene was developed and applied in China National Rice Research Institute. Sixteen genes have been cloned by Chinese scientists and many genes have been fine mapped so

1 Recent progress on rice Genetics in China by Hua Jiang, Long- Biao and Qian Qian in Journal of Integrative Plant Biology Vol 49 no 6 2007

2 Super hybrid rice breeding in China by Shi Hua Cheng, Li Yong Cao in Journal of Integrated plant Biology, 2007

far. It is expected that in the next decade the number of genes to be isolated and characterized will increase greatly.

4.6.2 Robotics and Artificial Intelligence

Early in 1999, Institution of Robotics BUAA brought forward a fish propulsion theory and the first bionic robot eel was created that had a maximum velocity of 0.6 m/s. Now the Institute of Robotics in BUAA is developing new kind of robot fish, which has high efficiency, high velocity and maneuverability.

There are several research groups in China working on bionic robot fish. The Institution of Automation, Chinese Academy of Science has ongoing projects on multiple robot fish cooperation and control. It focuses on the mechanism of the fish like motion and AI in fish robots. The Institution of Robotics in BUAA works on the mechanical structure and the driving system on robot fish and is working on the velocity, efficiency and stability. There is also a group studying on the hydrodynamics and mechanism of fish like swimming in the University of Science and Technology of China. Since the hydrodynamics of fish motion is not clear, it is difficult to make the fish move free. The Institution of Automation has adopted intelligent control into such a situation. The velocity is divided into two parts: orientation control and speed control. A method based on fuzzy control is proposed to adjust the error on motion direction and a neural network method is used to tune the oscillating frequency of the fish body to adjust the speed. A point-to-point algorithm is presented to control the fish to moving from one point to the other as straight as possible.*

The latest robot fish SPCII was completed in 2003. It uses the Global Positioning System to perambulate independently. The maximum velocity is 1.16 times of its full length, which would be the best in the world.

Robots are also been made to undertake work that is considered dangerous and risky for human beings such as fire fighting and

* Some Progress of Advanced Robotics in China-Report to JCF 2003 of IARP by Xianzhong DAI

anti terrorism activities. The Shenyang Institute of Automation has developed a tracked manipulator-integrated mobile platform, named WeiFu Robot to conduct anti-terrorism missions like explosive ordnance disposal, handling hazardous materials, urban search and rescue.

The National High-Tech Research and Development Programme launched the Human Robot project in 2001. Under this programme, the Beijing institute of technology developed the BHR-01 humanoid robot consisting of a head, two arms two legs and has a total of 33 Degrees of freedom. It has sensory devices including 26 axes force/torque sensors, 3 accelerometers and 3 gyro-sensors. The two-force/torque sensors are located on each foot to detect the contact between the feet and the ground. The accelerometer and the gyro-sensors are located in the body to estimate body acceleration and its inclination relative to the gravitational direction. These sensors are extremely important for the stable walk control of the BHR-01.

The Civil Aviation University of China and Tianjin YAAN Technology Electronics Co. Ltd have collaborated to create China's first mobile robotic guard on November 20, 2006. The robot is capable of locomotion over different types of surfaces including up to 20-degree inclination. It is also equipped with solar sensors that it uses for obstacle avoidance as it autonomously navigates.

Surgical robots are gaining in importance in the field of modern surgical technique. Surgical robots can help the surgeons perform the operation more accurately, more dexterously, without tremor and fatigue. They can reduce the operation time, minimize incision and shorten recovery time. Researchers in China are therefore focusing on this area of robotic research. The Beijing Institute of Technology has developed a mouth-orthopedic robot and the Shenyang Institute of Automation has developed a nose-orthopedic robot. The Institute of Robotics in BUAA has developed robot assisted frameless sterotactic neurosurgery system and has successfully applied in over 600 clinical applications. On September 10, 2003 the first remote operation of neurosurgery was conducted between Beijing and Shenyang. The remote telerobot assisted neurosurgery system is based on Li Yuan BH 600. The surgical robot has a 5 DOF and can be controlled by a doctor with a joystick. The patients' CT/MRI is transmitted to the surgeon through the e-mail and the wired model of calibrated robot, tumor, puncture path and head base line was overlaid on the video image to provide the doctor with augmented reality. The surgeon was in the Navy Hospital; Beijing while the patient was in Shenyang Center Hospital about 600 km away. This was the first remote operation in China and maybe in the world. It may be the first application of tele-surgery that takes advantage of video overlay technology to overcome the time delay that exists in communication through the Internet.

In industries, the demand for robotic automation is increasing–China is expected to need more than 100,000 robots by 2015 with the growing industrial automation. These would be used in the production of automobiles, engineering machinery, electric machines and electronic products. China began making robots in 1972, yet most of the robots in use are imported. In 2002, there were about 3,500 robots in use and about 80% of them were imported from countries like USA, Japan etc.[1]

4.6.3 Information Technology

The growth of ICT in the country has been remarkable since September 20, 1987 when Prof. Qian Tianbai of Hsing Hua University sent China's first email titled "Crossing the Great Wall to Join the World." This marked the beginning of the use of Internet in China. The Chinese Internet population has seen tremendous growth. According to the World Fact File, there were 162 million users in 2007. Subscription rates are growing at rate of 6% a month. There is however a digital divide among the population. About 70% of all the Internet users in China live in the big cities of Beijing, Shengai and Guangzhou in the eastern coast. The 13 provinces in western China have less than 1% users and vast parts of the western regions were not even connected.

1 "Robotics in greater demand in China" in People's Daily September 3, 2002.

China's competence in ICT is mainly concentrated on telecommunication, home appliances, computers and integrated circuits design. In January 2008, the Chinese Ministry of Information Industry published the 11th FYP (2006-2010) on five areas- integrated circuits, software, electronics, electronic basic material and key components and electronic special-purpose equipment and devices.

The Chinese manufactures are also looking towards the information technology sector to change the cheap, low quality made-in-China tag that the Chinese product have in the international markets. The Chinese manufacturers are investing in various softwares to enhance the quality of product management.

China has increased the spending in research and development in the sector. Since 1999, China R& D has increased more than 20% per year. In December 2006, China became the country with the second highest R&D investment in the world after US. China's domestic ICT industry will be stronger in the next five years as the country continues to upgrade its telecommunication infrastructure in its drive towards the global level of productivity.

4.6.4 Nanotechnology

According to a study in Beijing about nanotechnology in China, the market in nano technology was US$ 5.4 billion in 2005. This has been predicted to increase to US$ 31.4 billion in 2010 and US$ 144.9 billion by 2015. The main segments are nanomaterials, nano electronics, nano bio and nano life sciences- these already account for 70% of the turn over. China has the added advantage of starting early in the race for nanotechnology. She was one of the few countries that began exploring the new technology in the 1990's and now has highly skilled and competent research teams. The country has Research and Development network of three national centers and over 20 universities and institutions in nanotechnology. Besides this the country is rich in mineral and biological sources that are important for developing nanomaterials.

The rapid development in China's nanotechnology is due to the intervention of the Central Government. In 1990's nanotechnology was added to the list of priority technology and has had state funding through the National 863 HiTech R&D Plan. The Plan provides for huge investment in nano projects and the Government intends to transform the nanosector to make it comparable to China's microelectronics, telecom and other high tech sectors.

The market share (world market) in 2010 will be more than 6 percent and 16 percent by 2015. China has understood that to compete and become a world leader in nanotechnology depends on the new and improved finished products. There are many major Chinese research centers and hundreds of enterprises that are involved in the production of nanotechnology in China. These are situated mainly around major economic centers such as Beijing, Shenyang, Shangai, Hangzhou and Hong Kong – accounting for 90% of all the nanotechnology R&D. It has become a multibillion-Yuan industry. China has become a world leader in terms of newly registered nano tech firms, public and related patents. In 2006, the number of companies in nanotechnology in China has reached 800.

In 2001, Shanghai government invested 30 million Yuan in nanotechnology-nano biology, nanomedicene and nanoelctronics; thus laying a solid foundation for nano sector. Presently the government is at the second stage of developing nano product industrialisation. By 2002 Shanghai had developed an extensive nanotech infrastructure, which led to the rapid development of nanotechnology in the years to come.

In Beijing, the Center for Nanotechnology at the Chinese Academy of Sciences was opened in 2001. The aim was to upgrade scientific co-operation while accelerating nanotechnology industrial development. A year later, in 2001 Beijing Tsinghua University announced a new approach to the production of carbon nanotubes at the rate of 15 kg per hour, which was 60 times faster than the original speed of production.

At present there are 30 institutions that are involved in basic nanotechnology research. In addition, Beijing, Shanghai and Shenzhen each have created their own R&D thereby uniting local R&D structure. In terms of basic nanotechnology R&D, China has reached the most advanced levels in the world, even comparable to the capacities of the United States.

All over the world attention is being paid to nanotechnology. Global research funding has increased rapidly and it is estimated to have touched US$ 8.6 billion in 2004. China ranks ninth in the world with US $111 million in 2004. All this investment has already yielding impressive results. China is now the third in the quality of nanoscience publications it produces, after US and Japan and second in the subfield of nanomaterials.

4.7 LINKAGES

The Government of China seems to recognize that higher growth almost always will lead to higher inflation. According to National Statistics Bureau, the rate of inflation of February is 8.7% - an 11 year high. Almost all of the increase is blamed on the sharply higher prices for meat and poultry which has seen a 49% increase since mid-2006. After the August 2007 inflation rates were released, the government froze all state controlled prices including petrol, water and electricity. In order to allay public anxiety, Beijing encouraged local governments to raise the minimum wages. However economists fear that this move could increase global inflation. It was the cheap labour that turned the country into world's factory. With the economic growth, the real wages of the workers have increased at double digits. Adding the increasing cost of raw materials, the cost of production has also increased. These costs will be passed on to the consumers worldwide. However, according to Standard Chartered economist, Gerard Lyons, China's move to more valuable manufactured goods such as automobiles would in years to come have the same effect on world markets as the country's push into low end manufacturing.

The main problem China is facing is to feed its millions, now and in the future. With about 43% of its population engaged in agriculture, it contributes only 11.3% to the GDP. The focus of Genetic engineering in China is therefore on developing better verities of rice and the scientists have been successful in their attempt too.

Robotics and artificial intelligence has also developed many applications for their technology ranging from explorations in Antarctica to medical robots. Similarly the government is promoting ICT in an attempt to connect the vast country together through the Internet.

Nanotechnology has grabbed the attention of the Chinese in a big way. With numerous publications to its credit, China has the support of the government to make it the next superpower. These technologies together would give China the boost to economy's growth rate as well as generate the required employment for the people.

5 SOUTH AFRICA

Capital — Pretoria
Area - 1,219,912 sq. km
Population — 48,782,759 (July 2008 estimate)
Average rate of growth of population — 0.828 %
Currency — rand (ZAR)
GDP(PPP) — $ 467.8 billion(2007)
GDP (per capita PPP) — $ 9,700 (2007)
GDP real growth rate — 5.1 % (2007)
Agriculture as a share of GDP — 3.2 % (2007)
Exports - $ 76.19 billion (2007)
Life Expectancy at birth — 48.89 years (2008 est)
Infant mortality rate - 45.11 deaths/1000 live birth (2008 est.)
Literacy — 86.4% (2003)
Human Development Index - 0.674 ranked 121st

The Republic of South Africa is located at the southern tip of the African continent. It is the largest economy in Africa and the 24th largest in the world. South Africa is often called the "rainbow nation", a term coined by Archbishop Desmond Tutu and later adopted by President Nelson Mandela to describe the country's multicultural diversity. South Africa has a generally temperate climate partly due to it being surrounded by the Atlantic and the Indian Oceans on three sides. South Africa covers 1.2 million sq. kms of land and the country completely surrounds the small kingdom of Lesotho. South Africa forms a distinct region divided from the rest of Africa by the rivers that mark its northern border. In the northwest the Orange River cuts through the Namib Desert and divides South Africa from Namibia. In the east the Limpopo Rivers separates the country from Zimbabwe and Botswana. Populations have moved across these rivers but generally the northern border region of the country is sparsely populated.

Majority of the people are engaged in the services sector (65%) contributing 70.9% to the GDP. Agriculture employs 9% of population and contributes 3.2% to the GDP. Water shortages are a chronic and severe problem in South Africa. The country has no commercially navigable rivers and no significant natural lakes. Along the coastlines there are several large lagoons and estuarine lakes. The government has created many artificial lakes mainly for the purpose of agriculture.

South Africa is one of the countries most affected by HIV, with 5.3 million HIV infected individuals. 20 % of the 15-49 year old population is infected, and in parts of the country more than 35% of women of childbearing age are infected. Overall, 11-12% of the population is infected. About 1,700 new infections occur each day, and approximately 40% of deaths are believed to be AIDS-related. There are approximately 660,000 children who have lost one or both parents, and by 2008 1.6 million children will have been orphaned by AIDS. Without effective prevention and treatment 5-7 million cumulative AIDS deaths are anticipated by 2010 (with 1.5 million deaths in 2010 alone), and there will be over 1 million sick with AIDS. The epidemic could cost South Africa as much as 17% in GDP growth by 2010. The extraction industries, education, and health are among the sectors that will be severely affected. A 2003 national operational plan provides the structure for a comprehensive response to HIV and AIDS, including a national rollout of antiretroviral therapy. This is the greatest challenge the country is facing today.

5.1 BRIEF HISTORY

The oldest evidence in the world documenting the emergence of humankind has been found in South Africa dating back at least 2.5 million years. Roughly 20,000 years ago, South Africa was occupied by people now known as San. Remnants of San communities still survive today as so-called Bushmen (now considered a pejorative term) in the Kalahari Desert. They were followed by the Khoikhoi, "men of men," or Khoi. Bantu-speaking Africans, whose descendants make up the overwhelming majority of the present-day inhabitants of South Africa, had moved south of the Limpopo River by about 1,500 years ago.

Portuguese mariners explored the west coast of Africa throughout the latter half of the fifteenth century. Two ships under Bartholomeu Dias eventually rounded the Cape of Good Hope in

1488 and in 1497; an expedition under Vasco da Gama rounded the Cape, sailed up the east African coast, and then crossed the Indian Ocean to India. Thus a way was opened for Europeans to gain direct access to the spices of the East without having to go through Arab middlemen.

In 1652, the Dutch East India Company (Verenigde Oostindische Compagnie—VOC) became the first settlers on the Cape. They came to establish a supply station in Table Bay on the Cape peninsula, instructing its station commander, Jan van Riebeeck, and his eighty company employees to build a fort and to obtain supplies of foodstuffs for the Dutch fleets. Within its first half decade, however, the Cape Colony was growing in ways unforeseen at its establishment. Van Riebeeck had concluded within two months of the establishment of the Cape settlement that slave labor would be needed for the hardest and dirtiest work. Some thought was given to enslaving Khoikhoi men, but the idea was rejected on the grounds that such a policy would be both costly and dangerous. In 1658, the VOC landed two shiploads of slaves at the Cape. Thereafter, all the slaves imported into the Cape until the British stopped the trade in 1807 were from East Africa, Mozambique, Madagascar, and South and Southeast Asia. The slave population, which exceeded that of the European settlers until the first quarter of the nineteenth century, was overwhelmingly male and was thus dependent on constant imports of new slaves to maintain and to augment its size.

In 1657 nine European men were released from the VOC's service, given the status of "free burghers," and were granted blocks of land. Conflict between Dutch farmers and Khoikhoi broke out as it became clear that the Dutch were there to stay and intended to encroach on the lands of the pastoralists. Many attempts were made to drive the Dutch away from the peninsula from 1659 and continued till1677. The final blow came in 1713, when a Dutch ship brought small pox to the Cape. The disease was not known in the Cape and left 90% of the population dead.

By the end of the century, pressures for land in and around the Cape peninsula had become intense. Fearing that the strategic port at Table Bay might fall into the hands of Napoleon, the British seized the Cape to defend their sea route to India and took over the Cape settlement in 1795.

A combination of local factors—population growth, the depletion of natural resources, and devastating drought and famine—led to revolutionary changes in the political, economic, and social structure of Bantu-speaking communities in southern Africa in the first half of the nineteenth century. Thousands of people died because of ecological catastrophe and warfare; thousands more were displaced. Large centralized states of tens of thousands of people with standing armies of up to 40,000 men and autocratic leaders emerged where before there had been only small-scale political entities and no chief had had total power. This period of revolutionary change—known as the *mfecane* (or crushing) by the Zulu and the *difaqane* by the Sotho—is also often referred to as "the time of troubles"

In 1807 Parliament in London ordered an end to British participation in the slave trade everywhere in the world. This decision threatened the basis of the Cape's labor supply, for farmers in the eastern areas as well as in the west.

Beginning in 1836, partly to escape British rule and cultural hegemony and partly out of resentment at the recent abolition of slavery, many Afrikaner farmers (Boers) undertook a migration known as the "Great Trek" to north and east into the African tribal territory where they established the republics of Transvaal and the Orange Free State.

The discovery of diamond and later gold deposits had tremendous impact on southern Africa. The export earning of the Cape Colony increased substantially and so did the population. Whereas the Cape's exports in 1870 had been worth little more than £2,000,000, with wool providing the bulk of earnings, by the end of the century the value of exports had risen to more than £15,000,000, with diamonds alone accounting for £4,000,000. Also there were close to 400,000 resident Europeans in the Cape Colony by 1900, twice the number who had lived there in 1865. Johannesburg, the newly established hub of this industry, had a population of 75,000 Europeans by the end of the century, which made it the largest city in southern Africa.

In 1872 a pass law was introduced that required all "servants" be in possession of passes that stated whether the holders were legally entitled to work in the city, whether or not they had completed their contractual obligations, and whether they could leave the city. This law became the foundation of the twentieth century South African pass laws and was enforced against the blacks only.

Other restrictions followed the pass law such as establishing special courts to process pass law offenders as rapidly as possible (the basis of segregated courts in the twentieth century), the laying out of special "locations" or ghettos in Kimberley where urban blacks had to live (the basis of municipal segregation practices), and, finally, in 1886 the formation of "closed compounds," fenced and guarded institutions in which all black diamond mine workers had to live for the duration of their labor contracts. The result of such practices was the highest rate of incarceration and the lowest living standards for urban blacks in the Cape Colony. South Africa's first industrial city thus developed into a community in which discrimination became entrenched in the economic and social order, not because of racial antipathies formed on the frontier, but because of the desire for cheap labor.

The final quarter of the nineteenth century was marked also by the rise of new forms of political and religious organization as blacks struggled to attain some degree of autonomy in a world that was rapidly becoming colonized. Since the right to vote was based on ownership of property, blacks could participate in electoral politics in increasing numbers in the 1870s and the 1880s, especially in the towns.

The South African War (1899-1902), fought by the British to establish their supremacy in South Africa and by the Afrikaners to defend their autonomy, lasted three years and caused enormous suffering. Eventually the British won the war. The defeat led in 1910, to the formation of the Union of South Africa. Louis Botha, a Boer became the first Prime Minister.

Several pieces of legislation marked the establishment of the Union of South Africa as a state in which racial discrimination received official sanction. The Native Labour Regulation Act (No. 15) of 1911 made it a criminal offense for Africans, but not for whites, to break a labor contract. Most important, the Natives Land Act (No. 27) of 1913 separated South Africa into areas in which either blacks or whites could own freehold land: blacks, constituting two-thirds of the population, were restricted to 7.5 % of the land; whites, making up one-fifth of the population, were given 92.5 %. The act also stated that Africans could live outside their own lands only if employed as laborers by whites. In particular, it made illegal the common practice of having Africans work as sharecroppers on farms in the Transvaal and the Orange Free State. All these pro-white policies led to the resistance from the blacks and organized political activity among Africans began with the establishment of the African National Congress in 1912.

In August 1914, Louis Botha and Jan Smuts, amid much controversy, took South Africa into World War I on the side of the British. Many attempts were made against Botha's government but were crushed by the armed forces. In the context of postwar depression, the mine owners in 1922 proposed that wages be reduced, and that the statutory "colour bar" be lifted, thereby enabling the employers to increase the ratio of black workers to white. The white workers, supported by the Labour and National parties, went on strike and in the ensuing conflict, seventy-six people were killed and more than four thousand were arrested. The new government took immediate steps to protect the white labour rights through various Acts.

World War II had a profound effect on South Africa, economically and socially. Between 1935 and 1945, the number of people employed in the manufacturing sector increased by 60%. By 1946, there were more Africans in the towns and cities than whites. Such developments contradicted the segregationist thinking that blacks should live in the rural areas and not become permanent urban residents. The population Registration Act, 1950 provided the basis for the segregation of the people of South Africa according to their races. The African National Congress was banned in 1960 and its leader, Nelson Mandela sentenced to life imprisonment. Protests against the apartheid intensified. In 1973, the UN declared apartheid "a crime against humanity" and in 1977, declared mandatory the existing embargo on the sale of arms to South Africa. The late 1970's and 1980's were marked by many military interventions. During this time the matter of demographics loomed large. While whites accounted for 21% of the population in 1936, by 1980, they constituted only 16% and future projections estimated the white population to be only 10%. In 1983, Botha's government proposed that power be shared among the whites, coloured and Indians with separate houses of parliament for each racial group. This created angry opposition from the National Party.

A need for change was felt by the National Party. In 1990, the President announced the un-banning of ANC and other anti-apartheid group, and Nelson Mandela was released from prison. In 1991, the Group Areas Act, the Land Acts and the population Registration Act, considered as the "pillars of apartheid" were abolished. A new constitution came to force in December 1993. The country's first non-racial elections were held in 1994 and Nelson Mandela became President on May 10, 1994.

In 1997, the Truth and Reconciliation Commission was set up to heal the wounds of apartheid and began hearings on human rights violations between 1960 and 1993. President Mandela concentrated on national reconciliation, seeking to forge a single South African identity and sense of purpose among a diverse and splintered populace, driven by years of conflict. The diminution of political violence after 1994 and its virtual disappearance by 1996 were testament to the abilities of Mandela to achieve this difficult goal.

Nelson Mandela retired in 1999 and after the national elections, Thabo Mbeki became the President. In his first term Mbeki had to deal with a slumping economy and a high crime rate. The country has the highest number of HIV positive people in the world. Efforts to control the epidemic were hit by the controversial views of the President who denied the link between HIV and AIDS. The international community and the African leaders condemned Mbeki's stance. In April 2004 elections, the ANC won a landslide victory and Mbeki was reelected for his second term. The government had promised to reduce poverty, stimulate economic growth and fight crime. However the government could not complete its term under Mbeki. Until the next elections in 2009, Kgalema Motlanthe has been appointed the President.

5.2 GOVERNMENT AND POLITICAL CONDITIONS

South Africa is a multiparty democracy with powers shared between the President and the parliament. The Parliament consists of two houses- the National Assembly and the National Council of Provinces. The National Assembly currently has 400 members elected by a system of "list proportional representation" where each party appearing on the ballot submits a rank-ordered list of candidates. The voters then cast their ballots for a party. The National Council of Provinces consists of 90 members- 10 from each of the nine provinces. It was created to give greater voice to the provincial interests. The Council must approve legislation that involves shared national and provincial competencies.

The President is the Head of the State. The National Assembly reelected Thabo Mbeki as President on April 14, 2004.The President has however resigned on 25th September 2008, and Kgalema Motlanthe is currently serving the remainder of his term. The next election is to be held on April 2009. The President works with his deputy president and the cabinet. Currently there are 28 ministers in the cabinet. On June 14, 2005 the deputy president was "removed" from office following corruption charges. The former Minister for Minerals and Energy, Phumzile Mlambo-Ngcuka was named Deputy President, making her the first women to hold the office.

The third part of the government is an independent judiciary. The Constitutional Court is the highest court for interpreting and deciding the constitutional matters while the Supreme Court of Appeal is the highest court for non-constitutional matters. The

Constitution provides the right for a fair, public trial within reasonable time of being charged and the right to appeal to a higher court. The bill of rights also guarantees the fundamental political and social rights of South African citizens.

5.3 ECONOMY

South Africa has a two- tiered economy- one that can rival the developed countries of the world; while the other tier only has the bare basic infrastructure. The country is therefore a productive, industrial economy that exhibits various characteristics of a developed economy. The formal sector with mining, manufacturing, agriculture and the services sector are highly developed. At the same time, there is a highly unequal distribution of wealth. When the country began its transition to a democratic, nonracial government in early 1990's, a policy was required that could strike a balance between sustained growth and decreasing socioeconomic disparities created by apartheid. To address this need, the Reconstruction and Development Programme was launched to improve conditions of the millions of population by providing housing, education, health care etc.

In order to demonstrate its commitment to open markets and privitisation, the government released the Growth, Employment and Redistribution strategy (GEAR). The strategy had mixed success. Budgetary reforms such as the Medium Term Expenditure Framework and the Public Finance Management Act that aims at better reporting, auditing and increased accountability have created transparency and predictability and have been widely acclaimed. Although the strategy brought greater financial discipline and macroeconomic stability, it failed to deliver in key areas. Formal employment continued to fall and the country's wealth remains very unequally distributed along racial lines. Trade liberalization also has progressed substantially since the early 1990s. South Africa has reduced its import-weighted average tariff rate from more than 20% in 1994 to 7% in 2002. These efforts, together with South Africa's implementation of its World Trade Organization (WTO) obligations and its constructive role in launching the Doha Development Round, show South Africa's acceptance of free market principles.

5.3.1 Population

South Africa has a population of 48,782,756 (July 2008 est.), and faces a growth rate of population (0.828 %)1 Literacy is 86.4% for the country as a whole. The country has an HDI ranking of 121 out of 177 countries listed by UN. The Human Poverty Index for developing countries ranks South Africa 55th among 108 countries. The median age of the population is 24.2 years making it one of the young countries of the world. However the infant mortality rate is very high in South Africa(45.11 deaths per thousand live births)

5.4 SECTORAL GROWTH

5.4.1 Agriculture

South Africa has a dual agricultural economy, with both well-developed commercial farming and more subsistence-based production in the deep rural areas. Covering 1.2-million square kilometers of land, South Africa is one-eighth the size of the United States and has seven climatic regions, from Mediterranean to subtropical to semi-desert. This biodiversity, together with a coastline 3,000 kilometers long and served by seven commercial ports, favours the cultivation of a highly diverse range of marine and agricultural products, from deciduous, citrus and subtropical fruit to grain, wool, cut flowers, livestock and game.

Agricultural activities range from intensive crop production and mixed farming in winter rainfall and high summer rainfall areas to cattle ranching in the bushveld and sheep farming in the arid regions. Maize is most widely grown, followed by wheat, oats, sugar cane and sunflowers.

---

1 World Fact File, Country studies-South Africa

While 13% of South Africa's land can be used for crop production, only 22% of this is high-potential arable land. The most important limiting factor is water availability. Rainfall is distributed unevenly across the country, with some areas prone to drought. Almost 50% of South Africa's water is used for agriculture, with about 1.3-million hectares under irrigation.

Today, South Africa is not only self-sufficient in virtually all major agricultural products, but is also a net food exporter. Farming remains vitally important to the economy and development of the southern African region. Since 1994, the government has been working to develop small-scale farming to boost job creation.

South Africa is the world's top exporter of avocados, tangerines and ostrich products, the second-biggest exporter of grapefruit, third-biggest exporter of plums and pears, and fourth-biggest exporter of table grapes. Farming contributes some 8% to the country's total exports. The largest export groups are wine, citrus, sugar, grapes, maize, fruit juice, wool, and deciduous fruit such as apples, pears, peaches and apricots.

South African Exports						
	1999	2000	2001	2002	2003	Ave.
Total SA products (millions)	R165	R210	R245	R315	R275	R242
Total agricultural products (miilions)	R14.8	R15.8	R20.1	Rs25.5	R23.0	R19.8
Agriculture as % of total exports	8.95	7.53	8.18	8.08	8.37	8.18

Source: Department of Agriculture

Primary agriculture accounts for about 4% of the gross domestic product. Major crops include citrus and deciduous fruits, corn, wheat, dairy products, sugarcane, tobacco, wine, and wool. South Africa has many developed irrigation schemes and is a net exporter of food.

South Africa and WTO Though South Africa was a founding member of the General Agreement on Tariffs and Trade (GATT), it participated little in trade negotiations as long as its government remained embroiled in domestic conflicts. Following the end of apartheid in 1994, however, South Africa began to actively voice the concerns of developing countries in the WTO. It now considers the Doha Development Round of world trade talks to be essential for accelerating development and increasing the scope of the developing world to bargain on its key issues. At the WTO ministerial meeting in Cancun in November 2003, South Africa led the coalescence of a new trade block of twenty articulate developing countries, along with India, Brazil, and China. The group came together over their insistence that they could not consider further lowering their import tariffs until developed countries, particularly the US and EU, committed to significantly lowering their subsidies of domestic agriculture production and export. The G20's rejection of the investment issues that the developed countries wanted to include in the negotiations and its insistence on prioritizing agriculture brought about the early ending of the Cancun meetings and has shifted the course of the Doha Development Round.

Together with Brazil, South Africa has advocated for access to affordable medicines, coming up against the United States and other rich countries seeking to protect their pharmaceutical industries and the intellectual property rights they claim provide the incentives for the invention of new treatments. These developed countries reluctantly accepted a decision made at Doha in 2001 that, when public health was at stake, recognized the right of WTO members to dismiss patents on expensive Western drugs and make generics themselves. These generics, however, could only be used domestically and not exported. A country without a drug industry would be no better off, being able neither to make inexpensive drugs itself nor to buy them from another country.

This problematic loophole was resolved in September 2003 before the Cancun meeting in an agreement that set up a framework for parallel importing of generic drugs between developing countries. This promises to stimulate the generic drug industry in South Africa, as well as expand the current ones in Brazil and

India. However, there are currently no plans in any country to issue licenses for generic production and export, perhaps due in part to the regulatory barriers and political pressures from developed countries that these generic industries still face.

As a member of the Cairns Group of agricultural exporting economies, South Africa is eager to see the export of agricultural and food products to developed countries facilitated by the lowering of tariff and non-tariff barriers, the elimination of export subsidies, and the maximum possible reduction in trade-distorting domestic support. Like the rest of its developing country and agriculture-exporting allies, South Africa is highly critical of the U.S.'s agricultural export subsidies and especially the EU's Common Agricultural Policy (CAP), and has repeatedly highlighted these concerns in trade negotiations.

Coined by the United Nations Security Council, the term "conflict diamonds" means rough diamonds used by rebel movements or their allies to finance conflict aimed at undermining legitimate governments. South Africa continues to play a key role in the Kimberley Process, a campaign to exclude conflict diamonds from the legitimate trade by introducing a certification scheme. Based in Johannesburg, tasks of the process range from tracing diamonds held by customs officials around the world, to informing countries and organizations on how to join the effort. Most WTO countries have joined the 74-country membership of the Kimberly Process, but it remains a priority to engage all WTO members, thereby facilitating uniform regulation of the diamond trade.

South Africa is eager to move ahead in world trade negotiations in order to avoid the potential alternative scenario of increased bilateral agreements and further marginalization of poor countries. Hashing out South Africa and the rest of the G-20's demands on agriculture with the U.S. and EU's political considerations and economic strength will be the most challenging task for the Doha Development Round.

5.4.2 Industry

South Africa has rich mineral resources. It is the world's largest producer and exporter of gold and platinum and also exports a significant amount of coal. During 2000, platinum overtook gold as South Africa's largest foreign exchange earner. The value-added processing of minerals to produce ferroalloys, stainless steels, and similar products is a major industry and an important growth area. The country's diverse manufacturing industry is a world leader in several specialized sectors, including railway rolling stock, synthetic fuels, and mining equipment and machinery.

South Africa's transportation infrastructure is well developed, supporting both domestic and regional needs. The Johannesburg International Airport serves as a hub for flights to other southern African countries. The domestic telecommunications infrastructure provides modern and efficient service to urban areas, including cellular and Internet services. In 1997, Telkom, the South African telecommunications parastatal, was partly privatized and entered into a strategic equity partnership with a consortium of two companies, including SBC, a U.S. telecommunications company. In exchange for exclusivity to provide certain services for 5 years, Telkom assumed an obligation to facilitate network modernization and expansion into unserved areas. The government is evaluating a proposal to establish a second network operator to compete with Telkom across its spectrum of services. Three cellular companies provide service to over 9 million subscribers.

South Africa's GDP is expected to increase gradually during the next few years, and in 2005 the government revised upward its 2005 estimated growth to 4.3%. Annual GDP growth between 1994 and 2004 averaged 3.0%. In 2003, real GDP growth slowed to a rate of 2.8%, but increased to 3.7% in 2004. The government estimates that the economy must achieve growth at a minimum of 6% to offset unemployment, which is estimated at 28%, although unofficial sources put it as high as 41%. In an effort to boost economic growth and spur job creation, the government has launched special investment corridors to promote development in specific regions and also is working to encourage small, medium, and micro-enterprise development. One of the great successes of the ANC government has been to get consumer inflation, which had been running in the double digits for over 20 years, under control. By 1998, inflation had fallen to 6.9%, and in 1999 and 2000 inflation was running at less than 6.0%. The rand's rapid depreciation in late 2001, however, led to greater inflationary pressure, causing 2002 inflation of 9.2%. The South African government cut the inflation rate to 4% in 2004, and the rand appreciated 39% from 2002 to 2004. The South African Reserve Bank increased interest rates and along with the 28% rand appreciation in 2003 led a reduced consumer inflation of 5.8%. The government also has made inroads into reducing the fiscal deficit and increasing foreign currency reserves. The government deficit was 1.1% of GDP in 2002 and 2.6% in 2003. The government's 2005 budget called for a moderate increase in spending to promote faster growth and poverty alleviation, while curbing budget deficits.

Exports reached 29.1% of GDP in 2007, up from 11.5% a decade ago. South Africa's major trading partners include the United Kingdom, the United States, Germany, Italy, Belgium, and Japan. South Africa's trade with other Sub-Saharan African countries, particularly those in the southern Africa region, has increased substantially. South Africa is a member of the Southern African Customs Union (SACU) and the Southern African Development Community (SADC). In August 1996, South Africa signed a regional trade protocol agreement with its SADC partners. The agreement was ratified in December 1999, and implementation began in September 2000. It intends to provide duty-free treatment for 85% of trade by 2008 and 100% by 2012.

5.4.3 Financial Institutions

South Africa has a sound financial institutional set-up that is comparable to the industrialized countries. The country has dozens of domestic and foreign institutions providing all kinds of services-commercial and retail merchant banking, mortgage lending, insurance and investment. Foreign banks are well represented and the country has extensive electronic banking facilities, ATM's as well as Internet banking. The National Payment System Act of 1998 was introduced in order to bring South African financial settlement system in line with the international practice on settlement systems and risk management procedures. Investment and merchant banking remain the most competitive front in the industry, while the country's four main banks- Absa, First National Bank, Standard bank and Nedbank retain their hold on the retail market.

5.4.4 Foreign Direct Investment

South Africa has a sound macro-economic policy, solid financial system possess infrastructure comparable to the developed countries and a sophisticated market. Inspite of all this, the country is struggling to attract foreign investment since it emerged from its apartheid isolation era in early 1990's. Foreign investment has only been a trickle amounting to just 0.5% of GDP in the last two years. This is well below what the country needs in order to make up for its low saving rate and low capital investment rate. The main reasons given for the poor performance of the country are related to the low growth rate of the economy, the small size of the market, distance from the world markets, and the hesitant privatization programme of the government.

The country is widely regarded as the entry point for the sub continent, but the region is small. Much as higher growth would push aside other concerns for investors, the South African cost base for manufacturers is not helped by the relatively small size of the domestic market, the transportation cost to world markets, the import parity pricing practiced by many raw material manufacturers, and the high cost of ICT services. The government has been, at best, hesitant about privatization and the only sell off of any significant size has been that of the state telco, Telkom. There are no heavy fiscal pressures from losses at state owned enterprises to accelerate privatisation and the signal from government now is that the transport parastatal, Transnet, and the electricity supply body, Eskom, are viewed as means for investment to promote growth.

Challenges Ahead: South Africa's post-apartheid governments have made remarkable progress in consolidating the nation's peaceful transition to democracy. Programs to improve the delivery of essential social services to the majority of the population are underway. Access to better opportunities in education and business is becoming more widespread. Nevertheless, transforming South Africa's society to remove the legacy of apartheid will be a long-term process requiring the sustained commitment of the leaders and people of the nation's disparate groups.

The Truth and Reconciliation Commission (TRC), chaired by 1984 Nobel Peace Prize winner Archbishop Desmond Tutu, helped to advance the reconciliation process. Constituted in 1996 and having completed its work by 2001, the TRC was empowered to investigate apartheid-era human rights abuses committed between 1960 and May 10, 1994; to grant amnesty to those who committed politically motivated crimes; and to recommend compensation to victims of abuses. In November 2003, the Government began allocation of $4,600 (R 30, 000) reparations to individual apartheid victims. The TRC's mandate was part of the larger process of reconciling the often conflicting political, economic, and cultural interests held by the many peoples that make up South Africa's diverse population. The ability of the government and people to agree on many basic questions of how to order the country's new society will remain a critical challenge.

One important issue continues to be the relationship of provincial and local administrative structures to the national government. Prior to April 27, 1994, South Africa was divided into four provinces and 10 black "homelands," four of which were considered independent by the South African Government. Both the interim constitution and the 1997 constitution abolished this system and substituted nine provinces. Each province has an elected legislature and chief executive—the provincial premier. Although in form a federal system, in practice the nature of the relationship between the central and provincial governments continues to be the subject of considerable debate, particularly among groups desiring a greater measure of autonomy from the central government. A key step in defining the relationship came in 1997 when provincial governments were given more than half of central government funding and permitted to develop and manage their own budgets. However, the national government exerts a measure of control over provinces by appointing provincial premiers.

Although South Africa's economy is in many areas highly developed, the exclusionary nature of apartheid and distortions caused in part by the country's international isolation until the 1990s have left major weaknesses. The economy is now in a process of transition as the government seeks to address the inequities of apartheid, stimulate growth, and create jobs. Business, meanwhile, is becoming more integrated into the international system, and foreign investment has increased dramatically over the past several years. Still, the economic disparities between population groups are expected to persist for many years, remaining an area of priority attention for the government.

5.5 EMERGING TECHNOLOGIES IN SOUTH AFRICA

South Africa has taken to genetically engineered crops in a big way. Along with supportive economic and intellectual property rights as well as biosafety policies GE crops have rapidly spread through the country. Approximately 100 million rands have been spend on biotechnology research and development. Over 600 biotechnology research projects exists at present in the sectors of medical, pharmaceuticals, agriculture, plants, beverages, chemicals and biosafety. In 1999, over 2, 50,000 hectares of land were planted with such crops. In 2000 this increased by 1, 00,000 hect. i.e., a 50 percent increase in a year. The first two crops released in the country were –pest resistant cotton and pest resistant maize crop. Later the South African government released genetically engineered white maize for human consumption. The country however has no legal provision for labeling so the genetically engineered crops are not labeled as such.

As Raymond K Bokor, agro-ecological technician, Ghana states that the multi national companies are flooding the market with genetically engineered seeds. The most affected are the poor farmers who cannot afford these new variety seeds, the technology and the chemicals required for them. Moreover the technology has come up with sterile seeds so that the farmers have to rely on the companies for the next sowing seeds and cannot use the previous harvest seeds. South Africa with its strong commercial market and good agricultural infrastructure has made it easy to introduce new variety of seeds. The country has a vocal and active scientific community that has led to a rapid expansion of genetic technology. Few products have been developed locally and approximately 100 million rands have been spend on biotechnology research and development. Over 600 biotechnology research projects exist in various fields-medical and pharmaceuticals, agriculture/plant, environment, food and beverages, chemical, veterinary and bio-safety. About 55 companies are involved in the technology. The uptake of the country is considered to be one of the fastest in the world.

Cloning in South Africa was not allowed until 2003 the National Health Bill has set certain criteria for human cloning – embryo stem cell research and therapeutic cloning. Reproductive cloning is still not permitted.

Any development, use, production or application of genetically modified organisms in South Africa is regulated by the Genetically Modified Organism Act, 1997. Although the Act made no reference to the labeling of products containing GMO's, on January 2004, the government adopted the 'Regulations governing the labeling of foodstuffs obtained through certain techniques of genetic modification'. Food containing GMO"S now require labeling if their composition, nutritional value, mode of storage or cooking is significantly different from the conventional food, if they contain genes that are known to cause allergies or if they contain genes from animals to humans.

5.5.1 Robotics and Artificial Intelligence

An eight-robot intersection in South Africa is the country's first solar powered traffic signal. The aim is to see if solar power can keep the robots functioning normally. These environment friendly robots can even add excess energy to the National Grid. The Central

Energy Fund has already committed to install solar powered robots in the important intersections around South Africa. 1

According to Keith Campbell, South Africa is lagging in research and development as well as education regarding robotics. The University of Kwazulu Natal is one of the leading institutions in robotics and mechatronics. There seems to be an educational gap in these subjects and the University is looking to educate students in systems education that is mechatronics. Prof. Glen Bright, head of School of Mechanical Engineering says that in terms of research and development robotics and mechatronics are in their initial stages because many academic have not been exposed to the technoiogy associated with them. Unfortunately the university is not receiving any support from the industry either. 2

5.5.2 Information Technology

South Africa was placed 37th out of 115 countries by the World Economic Forum's Global Information Technology Report 2005/06 for its overall ICT readiness. It is placed ahead of countries such as China, Greece, Italy and India.

Another project launched in 2007 to open the digital world to South Africa is called 'The Digital Doorway'. It is seen as an alternative means to promote computer literacy in the villages. Since its launch 150 terminals have been installed. The first such programme was set up in 2002 and involved setting up a free standing multimedia computer terminal with a keyboard and a touch pad embedded in a kiosk, accessible to the people 24 hrs a day. The project is a joint initiative of the Department of Science and technology, the Center for Scientific and Industrial Research and state owned power utility Eskom. The aim is to provide people in the rural and disadvantaged areas with computer equipment to experiment and learn with minimal external input. The terminals have the regular word processing software and also have

1 "Solar robots to show the way" by Thabang Mokopanele Jan 2008

2 "Lack of exposure to robotics and mechatronics now biting" by Keith Campell December 2007

mathematics, science, music and language applications, HIV/AIDS presentations, Internet and entry level versions of Microsoft Word and Excel. Within a month of installation 60% of the children had already taught each other basic computer functions. In addition the terminals are equipped with satellite receivers and general radio service cellular data technology for updating content and to monitor user feedback.

Another major achievement in bridging the digital divide is the creation of the first all-South African language keyboard. Translate.org.za has released the popular word processing, spreadsheet and presentation software web browser and e-mail programme in all 11 official languages. According to its founder, Dwayne Bailey this is the first Africans-helping-Africans, no strings attached free software. The launch of this software meant that language was no longer a barrier and more than 20% of South Africans who were not fluent in English could use computers in their own language. The organization won the African ICT Achiever 2006 Award for bridging the digital divide in Africa.

The government of South Africa has placed great emphasis on ICT sector development the country has an extensive National ICT strategy that addresses ICT penetration especially the disadvantaged sections of the people. The government has created the State Information Technology Agency to encourage the provision of information technology, information systems and related services in a managed secure environment. In addition, the government has launched Info.com 2025, which serves as a collective programme of ICT projects designed to establish a networked information community and make South Africa globally competitive. Info.com 2025 addresses issues of policy, infrastructure, human capacity and local content within ICT industries.

One of the main problems facing ICT in South Africa is the 'brain drain' of her technical and entrepreneurial skilled people. An estimated 200-300 ICT skilled personnel are leaving the country every month. This is caused by high growth of demand for ICT world wide and low remuneration in the home country. Inspite of high unemployment rates of 30-35%; it is difficult to find skilled

ICT manpower. In order to address this problem, the government has set up a Human Resource Development Fund. This Fund is being used to provide grants and subsidies to promote adequately skilled human resources for ICT. The Department of Education has responded by launching SchoolNet- a strategic partnership linking the school and the Internet.

Three important taskforces have been introduced to use ICT for social and economic development. They include the Presidential International Task Force on Information Society and Development (to focus mainly on global ICT markets), the National IT Task Force (which will deal with the issue of "brain drain" and the deployment of ICT initiatives locally) and the IT Council (to handle local and provisional government IT functions). In addition, the government has announced the establishment of the Investment Council that will focus on positioning South Africa's imports and exports globally and also on generating foreign direct investment through international collaborations.

International aid has also come in to boost the ICT sector. On February 2008, Finland has pledged R138 million (12 million Euros). The funds will enhance the delivery and implementation of ICT infrastructure in the Limpopo and Northern Cape provinces over the next three years.

5.5.3 Nanotechnology

Although South Africa may be a late entrant in this technological race, it has many possibilities in nanotechnology. South African scientists are using nano technology to develop new health care tools, advanced materials and energy technologies. Research is underway at South Africa's first two Nanotechnology Innovation Centers based at Mintek- the country's National Mineral Research Organization and the National Center for nano-structured materials at the Council for Scientific and Industrial Research in Pretoria. CSIR scientists are already working on projects in advanced material manufacturing and energy. 1

1 "South Africa gets nanotech underway" in Science and Development Network, January 11, 2008

A recent South African strategy document outlines two possibilities in nano technology for South Africa. Nanotechnology can add immense value to the African minerals such as gold, platinum, palladium, titanium and so on. The other focus is the role of nanotech in reducing poverty. The technology can be used to develop low cost energy, low cost electronics.

Africa has distinct opportunities for applications of South Africa's University of Zululand work on energy storage and water treatment. The Department of Chemistry is focusing on Coordinate Chemistry that studies how well the disparate chemicals come together in various combinations. The team is developing a variety of organometallic compounds, some for use as organic anti-biotics and others for treating chloroquine-resistant malaria Compounds are also being investigated for possible uses as microelectronic devices, and in treating industrial wastewater polluted with heavy metals. The synthesis and characterization of nanomaterials for possible industrial applications puts the University in a leadership position. The materials on the ultrasmall nanomaterial shows unique properties that useful for various applications in light emitting devices used in medicine (laser sensors etc.) the team is making nanoparticles in the top-down approach where something big is taken and broken down chemically to produce nanoparticles. This approach is environment friendly is of high quality and avoids the use of volatile and toxic compounds that are used in the other methods.

5.6 LINKAGE

South Africa has great potential in the emerging technology applications. The country has taken to genetic engineering in a great way. However robotics and artificial intelligence has yet to catch up in the country. There is a need to find alternative uses of the technology, such as the use of nanotechnology in adding value to the minerals of gold, platinum and titanium. The growth rate has increased from 1.9 % in 2004 to 5.00% in 2008. However the country needs to make use of the new and emerging technologies to create more employment for the people. The country has high unemployment rate of 23% and an increasing inflation-from 5.9% in 2004 to 6.50% in 2008.

CONCLUSION

The BRICS have achieved substantial growth rates in these years. However the current financial crisis has set a damper on the growth rates of these economies. According to economists, the BRICS have been affected by the financial meltdown of October 2008. In 2007-2008, the banking sector of the developed countries was rocked by a financial crunch triggered by the collapse of sub-prime mortgage in the USA. In August-October 2008, the crisis led to the financial meltdown in the USA, Europe and other developed economies. The governments took unprecedented steps to prevent the financial system from collapse. Contrary to predictions of decoupling of the emerging economies from the developing countries, the BRICS were hit by the effects of the crisis. The foreign investors flew out of BRICS in fear of the global recession.

As the countries in the West prepare themselves for a period of recession in 2009, it is clear the BRICS will also face the effects of the global recession. Foreign investment would slow down. This would adversely the foreign direct inflow of investment that played an important role in the growth of the emerging economies. The recession has also affected the consumer demand across the world. China, Brazil and India would be worst affected. About two-third of China's exports are to the developed world. Brazil's exports of agricultural commodities – soy and coffee would similarly be affected. India's services sector accounts for more than half of GDP. The sector would be affected if the foreign outsourcing companies were forced to close or invest less. South Africa would also be affected.

According to economists, Russia would be the most vulnerable of the emerging economies to global recession as it is the least diversified. Russia is heavily reliant on hydrocarbon exports, accounting for about half of export revenues. Additionally the country is considered risky due to the summer war 2008 with Georgia and the escalating tension with the west.

The combined effects could lead to job losses and slower growth in the BRICS. Consumer spending that was to fuel growth during the recession is also slowing down. The BRICS however have their strengths that could help them to come out of the financial crisis. These countries have substantial foreign exchange reserves that allow their governments to boost public spending in order to support the economy. Moreover, the previous decades of growth has build up a strong consumer demand that could lead as the prime engine of growth for the economy. The crisis is also expected to remove the danger of inflation, making life easier for the emerging economies' consumers and allow the government to ease the interest rates fuelling further growth.

The emerging economies have the advantage of the emerging technologies to use and become the superpowers of the future. However there are dangers associated with becoming dependant on each of the technologies. The future may well be determined by how these challenges are dealt with. For example, molecular nano-technology will enable the construction of a bacterium scale self-replicating mechanical robots that can feed on organic materials. A person with malicious intend in possession of this technology may cause the extinction of intelligent life on earth. Similarly in creating the first super intelligent entity, suppose a mistake was made and the goals given was to annihilate mankind. The consequences can be easily imagined. The fabulous advancements in genetic technology may make it possible for a terrorist or lunatic to create a doomsday virus, and hold the world to ransom. The technologies therefore have their limitations and the emerging economies need to approach them with caution.

The right combination of the technologies with the resources available with the countries would enable the BRICS to get back on the growth track and lead the world to greater prosperity.

ABBREVIATIONS

ANATEL	—	National Telecommunication Agency, Brazil
ANC	—	African National Congress
ARCI	—	Advanced Research Center for Powder Metallurgy and New Materials, Hyderabad, India
BJP	—	Bharatiya Janta Party
BNDES	—	Brazilian Development Bank
CCP	—	Chinese Communist Party
CNTBio	—	National Technical Committee for Biosafety (Comissao Tecnica Nacional de Biosseguranca)
CVRD	—	Companhia Vale do Rio Doce— the largest Brazilian mining company
ECLAC	—	Economic Commission for Latin American and the Caribbean
EMBRAPA	—	Brazilian Agricultural Research Corporation
FDI	—	Foreign Direct Investment
FOSS	—	Free and Open Source Software
GDP	—	Gross Domestic Product
IBGE	—	Brazilian Statistical Institute
ICT	—	Information and Communication Technology
INC	—	Indian National Congress
KMT	—	Kuomintang, Nationalist party of China
KPRF	—	Kommunisticheskaya Partiya Rossiyskoy Federastsri –Russian anti—reform party
MICEX	—	Moscow International Currency Exchange
NPC	—	National People's Congress, China
NELP	—	New Exploration and Licensing policy
PPP	—	Purchasing Power Parity

PRC	—	People's Republic of China
R & D	—	Research and Development
ROC	—	Republic of China
SWAN	—	State Wide Area Network
UFRGS	—	Federal University of Rio Grande do Sul, Brazil
UN	—	United Nation
WTO	—	World Trade Organisation

REFERENCES

1. Aslund, Anders (2006),"Russia's WTO Accession", Testimony at the Hearing on EU Economic and Trade Relation with Russia, Brussels, November 21.
2. Aelaja, Tai (2007), "Weak property rights hold back Russian IT" in Moscow Times, March.
3. Bhattacharya, Dipankar (2006), "The Tata Corus Deal:hype and reality" in CPIML Newsletter-Liberation, December.
4. Cheng, Shin Hua & Li Yong Cao (2007), "Super Hybrid Rice Breeding in China: Achievements and Prospects" in *Journal of Integrative Plant Biology* Vol. 49, Issue 6, June. Blackwell Publishing, Shanghai.
5. da Motta Veiga, Pedro (2004),"FDI in Brazil: regulation, flows and contributions to development"-Investment Country Report, International Institute for Sustainable Development, May.
6. de Castro LAB (2004),"Strategy for obtaining social benefits from gene revolution" in Journal of Medical and Biological Research, July 2004.
7. Dai, Xianzhong (2003), "Some Progress of Advanced Robotics in China" Report to JCF of IARP
8. Dias, Antonio Flavio, Elza Angela B. Brito da Cunha & Levon Yeganiantz (2000), "The Economic Challenge of Biotechnology in Brazil" Paper presented for the Fourth International Conference of the International Consortium on Agricultural Biotechnology Research on "The Economics of Agricultural Biotechnology" Ravello (Italy), August 24-28.

9. Enbysk, Monte (2008) "Brazil's largest bank shows its new software to Ballmer" February 14, in http//www.microsoft.com/enable/news/brazil0299.aspx.
10. Jiang, Hua, Long-Biao & Qian Qian (2007) "Recent Progress on Rice Genetics in China" in *Journal of Integrative Plant Biology*, Vol 49, No 6.
11. Kausik, Vijay & Boris Yudin (1997)"Gene Therapy and Human Genome Project" in Eubios Journal of Asian and International Vol 7.
12. Mistry, Sharad (1999)"Indian labs working on 'terminator' technology" in Indian Express, January.
13. Ogutcu, Mehmet (2002) "Attracting FDI for Russia's modernization –battling against all odds" OECD-Russia Investment Roundtable, 19 June, Russia.
14. Pai, Uday Lal (2007), "India steps up to robotics" in Automation World http//www.automationworld.com/webonly-3129.
15. Rubin, Debra (2007)"Brazil holds fair to promote robots in Industries and Schools" in brazilmag.com, April.
16. Saneko, Alexandr (2007)"Nanotechnology to cure cancer in Russia" in Science http://en.mykinda.com/20/11/2007/nanotechnology-to-cure-cancer-russia
17. Swartz, Dan (2000), "Genetically Engineered Food and Crops in Russia", Report prepared by ANPED, The Alliance for Sustainability and SEU, Socio Ecological Union, Russia.
18. Tavernise, Sabrina (2003), "Russia Imposes flat tax on income and its coffers swell" New York Times, March 23.
19. Thuban, Dario (2007), "Russia to redirect billions in major nanotechnology push" in Space Mart, Moscow, June 6.
20. Trichet, Jean Claude (2007), "The Growing Importance of Emerging Economies in the Globalised World and its Importance for International Architecture", Speech delivered at the 10th LK Jha Memorial Lecture, RBI, Delhi.

BIBLIOGRAPHY

1. Bhat S.R, V.L Chopra, "Transgenic Crops: Priorities and Strategies for India" in Current Science Volume 88, No 6, March 25,2005.
2. Boker, Raymond.K., "Resistance to Genetic Engineering in Africa" Presented at Biodevastation , held in St. Missouri, May 2003
3. Botelo, Antonio. J., Jason Dedrick, Kenneth L Kraemer & Paulo B Tigre , "From Industry Protection to Industry Promotion- I T Policy in Brazil", Center for Research on IT and Organisation, Irvine, Paper 5,1999.
4. Bueno, Tania CD, Erica BQ Riberio, Hugo C Hoeschl, Samantha Hoffmann "E-Courts in Brazil –conceptual model for entirely electronic court process." Presented at 18th Conference BILETA: Controlled Information in the Online Environment ,April 2003, London
5. Dhlamini, Sizwe.M., Michael.O.Kanchienga & T.Marwala "Artificial Intelligence as an aide in management of security technology" in IEEEAfricon Paper 200, 2007.
6. Luis, Jose "Foreign Investment in Latin American and the Caribbean -2004 report to ECLAC, March 2005.
7. Ma, Hong, Kang Chong & Xing-Wang Deng (2007), "Rice Research: Past, Present and Future" in Journal of Integrative Plant Biology Volume 49, issue 6 2007.
8. Popelka, Carlos .J., Nancy Terryn & T.J.V Higgins "Gene Technology for Grain Legumes: Can it contribute to the food challenge in developing countries?" in Direct Science, Ireland, 2004.

9. Smith, Garry, "Towards efficiency in Brazilian agriculture" in The OECD Observer, number 207, August 1997.
10. Stankevich, Lev. A., "Intellectual robots in Russia- experience of development and RoboCup participation". Presented at the SPECOM '2004-9th Conference Speech and Computer, St. Petersburg, Russia, September 20-22, 2004.

APPENDIX

The Combined Table of Various Indicators among the BRICS–1965 to 2007

	Year Indicators	1965	1970	1975	1980	1985	1990	1995	2000	2001	2002	2003	2004	2005	2006	2007
Brazil	GDP	21.79	42.33	123.71	235.02	222.94	461.95	786.95	644.48	552.29	505.90	552.46	663.8	882.4	1067.82	1314.17
	Rate of growth of GDP	3.05	8.77	5.21	9.11	7.95	-4.30	4.40	4.29	1.32	2.61	1.27	5.72	2.90	3.72	5.42
	Population-total	0.084	0.095	0.108	0.122	0.136	0.149	0.162	0.174	0.177	0.179	0.182	0.184	0.187	0.189	0.192
	Population rate of growth	2.84	2.47	2.36	2.34	2.13	1.72	1.51	1.47	1.45	1.43	1.41	1.38	1.35	1.33	1.20
	Exports	1.69	2.98	9.33	21.27	20.31	37.88	55.80	64.31	67.28	71.32	82.79	109.03	133.50	156.49	168.93
	Exports as %of GDP	7.74	7.03	7.54	9.05	12.25	8.20	7.26	9.96	12.18	14.10	14.99	16.43	15.13	14.65	12.85
	Imports	1.21	3.15	14.24	26.58	32.16	67.48	63.48	75.67	74.54	63.66	66.71	83.29	101.79	125.11	140.16
	Imports as percentage of	5.56	7.45	11.51	11.31	7.10	6.96	8.78	11.74	13.50	12.58	12.08	12.55	11.54	11.72	10.67
	Foreign Direct Investment	—	0.39	1.30	1.91	1.41	0.99	4.86	32.78	22.46	16.59	10.14	18.17	15.19	18.78	—
	External Debt	—	5.73	27.33	71.52	103.61	119.73	160.47	241.55	229.02	230.92	234.82	219.50	187.30	194.15	—
Russia	GDP	—	—	—	—	—	516.81	395.53	259.71	306.60	345.48	431.49	591.74	764.53	990.58	—
	Rate of growth of GDP	—	—	—	—	—	-3	-4.14	10	5.09	4.74	7.35	7.14	6.4	7.4	8.1
	Population-total	—	—	—	—	—	0.148	0.148	0.146	0.145	0.145	0.144	0.143	0.143	0.142	0.141
	Population rate of growth	—	—	—	—	—	0.39	-0.13	-0.004	-0.241	-0.44	-0.48	-0.52	-0.49	-0.46	-0.61
	Exports						93.86	115.85	114.43	113.12	121.65	151.70	203.42	268.94	334.79	391.48
	Exports as percentage of GDP	—	—	—	—	—	18.16	29.29	44.06	36.89	35.21	35.15	34.37	35.17	33.80	30.32
	Imports						92.74	102.42	62.42	74.25	84.41	102.78	130.99	164.33	208.77	282.22
	Imports as percentage of GDP	—	—	—	—	—	17.94	25.90	24.03	24.22	24.43	23.82	22.14	21.50	21.08	21.87

Contd.

	Foreign Direct Investment	—	—	—	—	—	—	2.07	2.71	2.75	3.46	7.96	15.44	12.89	30.83	—
	External Debt	—	—	—	—	—	—	121.40	159.99	152.50	147.37	175.70	196.80	229.07	251.08	—
India	GDP	58.83	61.20	97.00	183.80	229.94	317.47	356.30	460.18	477.85	507.19	599.46	700.92	808.71	916.25	117.97
	Rate of growth of GDP	-2.41	5.15	9.14	6.74	5.23	5.29	7.57	4.03	5.22	3.77	8.37	8.28	9.24	9.69	9.02
	Population-total	0.487	0.548	0.613	0.687	0.765	0.850	0.932	1.016	1.033	1.049	1.064	1.079	1.095	1.109	1.123
	Population rate of growth	2.34	2.31	2.28	2.25	2.04	2.02	1.78	1.68	1.62	1.55	1.49	1.43	1.37	1.31	1.21
	Exports	1.97	2.34	5.54	11.42	12.22	22.65	39.08	60.88	60.97	73.47	88.75	126.65	160.84	202.37	249.71
	Exports as percentage of GDP	3.35	3.83	5.71	6.21	5.31	7.13	10.97	13.23	12.76	14.49	14.80	18.07	19.89	22.09	21.32
	Imports	3.10	2.40	6.52	17.19	17.78	27.14	43.33	65.13	65.22	78.52	96.49	139.31	183.74	230.02	286.15
	Imports as percentage of GDP	5.28	3.93	6.72	9.35	7.73	8.55	12.16	14.15	13.65	15.48	16.10	19.87	22.72	25.10	24:44
	Foreign Direct Investment	—	45.46	-10.33	79.16	106.1	236.7	2413.6	3584.2	5471.9	5620.0	4322.8	5771.3	6676.5	17453.1	—
	External Debt	—	8.42	13.85	20.69	40.95	83.63	94.46	99.09	98.48	105.02	112.85	124.38	123.13	153.08	—
China	GDP	69.71	91.51	161.16	188.24	304.91	354.64	728.01	1198.5	1324.8	1453.8	1640.9	1931.6	2243.8	2657.9	3280.1
	Rate of growth of GDP	16.36	19.4	8.7	7.8	13.5	3.8	10.9	8.4	8.3	9.1	10	10.1	10.4	11.6	11.9
	Population-total	0.72	0.82	0.92	0.98	1.05	1.13	1.20	1.26	1.27	1.28	1.29	1.29	1.30	1.31	1.32
	Population rate of growth	2.3	2.76	1.76	1.25	1.36	1.46	1.09	0.71	0.73	0.67	0.62	0.60	0.64	0.56	0.62
	Exports	—	2.39	7.39	20.17	30.49	67.97	167.97	279.56	299.41	365.39	985.00	655.83	863.89	1061.68	—
	Exports as a % of GDP	—	2.61	4.59	10.71	9.99	19.17	23.07	23.33	22.6	25.13	29.55	33.95	37.30	39.94	—
	Imports	2.47	7.36	20.86	43.09	55.54	151.88	190.32	271.33	328.01	448.92	606.54	712.09	852.77	—	—
	Imports as a %of GDP	—	2.70	4.57	11.08	14.13	15.66	20.86	20.92	20.48	22.56	27.36	31.40	31.74	32.08	—

Contd.

	Foreign Direct Investment	—	—	—	0.057	1.66	3.49	35.85	38.39	44.24	49.31	47.08	54.94	79.13	78.09	—
	External Debt	—	—	—	—	16.70	55.30	118.09	145.73	184.82	186.13	208.45	247.70	281.61	322.85	—
South Africa	GDP	10.97	17.85	36.95	80.71	67.07	112.01	151.11	132.88	118.48	110.87	166.65	216.44	242.05	254.99	277.58
	Rate of growth of GDP	8.72	5.25	1.69	6.62	-1.21	-0.32	3.11	4.15	2.74	3.67	3.12	4.84	5.10	4.99	4.80
	Population-total(in million)	19.83	22.09	24.73	27.58	31.31	35.20	39.12	44.00	44.81	45.25	45.80	46.34	46.89	47.39	47.59
	Population rate of growth	2.25	2.17	2.20	2.33	2.59	2.03	2.16	2.48	1.83	0.96	1.22	1.19	1.17	1.06	0.41
	Exports	2.91	3.89	10.23	28.56	21.07	27.15	34.41	37.03	35.69	36.58	46.76	57.69	66.52	76.11	84.08
	Exports as a % of GDP	26.48	21.80	27.69	35.38	31.42	24.24	22.77	27.87	30.13	32.99	28.05	26.55	27.48	29.85	30.29
	Imports	3.03	4.52	11.14	22.07	15.14	21.02	33.39	33.11	30.90	32.32	42.97	58.54	68.75	84.69	94.35
	Imports as a % of GDP	27.58	25.34	30.16	27.35	22.57	18.76	22.09	24.92	26.08	29.15	25.78	27.05	28.40	33.21	33.99
	Foreign Direct Investment	—	0.33	0.187	-0.01	-0.452	-0.075	1.25	0.97	7.27	0.735	0.783	0.701	6.52	-0.12	—
	External Debt	—	—	—	—	—	—	25.36	24.86	24.05	25.09	27.42	27.11	31.09	35.55	—

Source: *World Development Indicators, World Bank* at *http://ddp-ext.worldbank.org/ext/DDPQQ*

Note: GDP, Exports and Imports in US billion $

Foreign Direct Investment, External Debt measured in US billion $

Value of Exports and Imports measured in US $ and as a percentage of Gross Domestic Product.

Population in billion persons.

Table 1: Agricultural Output of Select Crops in China
(10 000 tons) source: National Bureau of Statistics, The People's Republic of China

Year	Rice	Pinang	Pine-apple	Mango	Sugar-cane	Tea	Peanuts	Banana
1991	181.9				453.6	2.1	8.4	19.7
1992	162.8				585.8	2.0	7.6	19.6
1993	182.0	13.7	27.7	21.7	480.3	2.1	7.6	21.3
1994	167.9	13.2	25.2	19.1	550.4	2.4	8.1	18.4
1995	168.7	15.6	25.6	20.8	486.2	2.1	9.2	17.3
1996	157.7	16.0	27.4	20.2	419.0	2.3	8.0	14.1
1997	166.3	15.6	30.1	21.0	390.2	2.4	8.4	20.5
1998	148.9	17.3	31.6	18.7	355.9	2.3	6.8	21.6
1999	155.9	17.0	34.8	20.7	325.6	2.1	6.7	21.3
2000	154.0	17.0	35.8	21.1	289.4	2.0	7.9	19.8
2001	139.6	16.5	38.9	21.3	218.0	2.0	5.6	20.5
2002	146.1	16.2	41.6	21.3	197.3	2.0	7.7	22.7
2003	133.8	16.0	44.8	22.1	169.6	2.1	7.3	22.3

http://www.allcountries.org/china_statistics/1_3_natural_resources.html

Yield of Farm (10,000 tons) Crops	1999	2000	2001	2002	2003	2004
Grain	50838.6	46217.5	45263.7	45705.8	43069.5	46946.9
Cereal	45304.1	40522.4	39648.2	39798.7	37428.7	41157.2
Rice	19848.7	18790.8	17758.0	17453.9	16065.6	17908.8
Wheat	11388.0	9963.6	9387.3	9029.0	8648.8	9195.2
Corn	12808.6	10600.0	11408.8	12130.8	11583.0	13028.7
Beans	1894.0	2010.0	2052.8	2241.2	2127.5	2232.1
Tubers	3640.6	3685.2	3563.1	3665.9	3513.3	3557.7
Oil-bearing Crops	2601.2	2954.8	2864.9	2897.2	2811.0	3065.9
Peanuts	1263.9	1443.7	1441.6	1481.8	1342.0	1434.2
Rapeseeds	1013.2	1138.1	1133.1	1055.2	1142.0	1318.2
Sesame	74.3	81.1	80.4	89.5	59.3	70.4
Cotton	382.9	441.7	532.4	491.6	486.0	632.4

Contd.

Fiber Crops	47.2	52.9	68.1	96.4	85.3	107.4
Jute and Ambary Hemp	16.4	12.6	10.6	15.9	10.0	8.7
Sugarcane	7470.3	6828.0	7566.3	9010.7	9023.5	8984.9
Beetroots	863.9	807.3	1088.9	1282.0	618.2	585.7
Tobacco	246.9	255.2	235.0	244.7	225.7	240.6
Flue-Cured Tobacco	218.5	223.8	204.5	213.5	201.5	216.3
Silkworm Cocoons	48.5	54.8	65.5	69.8	66.7	73.1
Mulberry Silkworm Cocoons	44.7	50.1	60.2	64.5	61.1	67.7
Tea	67.6	68.3	70.2	74.5	76.8	83.5
Fruits	6237.6	6225.1	6658	6952	15517	15340

Yield of Farm Crops per Hectare (kg/hectare)	1999	2000	2001	2002	2003	2004
Cereal	4945	4753	4800	4885	4873	5187
Cotton	1028	1093	1107	1175	951	1111
Peanuts	2961	2973	2888	3011	2654	3022
Rapeseeds	1469	1519	1597	1477	1582	1813
Sesames	1066	1034	1061	1180	863	1128
Jute and Ambary Hemp	2538	2516	2046	2868	2462	2719
Sugarcane	57338	57626	60625	64663	64023	65199
Beetroots	25334	24518	26807	30232	24925	30829
Flue-Cured Tobacco	1797	1763	1732	1792	1768	1889

Item		2004
Land Resources	(10 000 hectares)	
Area of Cultivated Land		13004
Area of Undeveloped Land		10800
Useable for Agricultural Production		3535
Area of Afforested Land		28493

Contd.

Undeveloped Land Usable for Afforestation		5471
Area of Grassland		40000
Utilizable Area		31333
Forest Resources		
Forest Area (10 000 hectares)		17491
Forest-coverage Rate (%)		18.21
Total Standing Stock Volume	(10 000 cu.m)	1361810
Stock Volume of the Forest	(10 000 cu.m)	1245585
Water Resources		
Land		
Total Water Resources Volume	(100 million cu.m)	24129.6
Surface Water Volume		23126.4
Ground Water Volume		7436.3
Duplicated Measurement between Surface Water and Groundwater		6433.1
Hydropower Resources	(100 million kw)	6.76
Developable Resources		3.79
Inland Water Area	(10 000 hectares)	1747
Cultivatable Area	675	
Cultivated Area	467	
Sea		
Theoretical Sea-energy Reserves	(100 million kw)	6.3
Coastal Area	(10 000 sq.km)	28
Sea-beach Area	(10 000 sq.km)	2.08
Area of Fishing Ground of Continental Shelf	(10 000 hectares)	28000
Cultivatable Area in Marine Areas	(10 000 hectares)	260.01
Cultivated Area		109.49
Cultivable Area in Shallow Sea and Sea-beaches	10 000 hectares)	242.00
Cultivated Area		89.37